ISBN 978-1-331-61309-1
PIBN 10212931

Idylls and Lyrics of the Nile ❧

By H. D. Rawnsley

London
Published by David Nutt
in the Strand
1894

TO MY FRIEND,

FRANCES POWER COBBE,

WITH TRUE REGARD

PREFATORY NOTE

WITH the exception of 'I.' and 'LIII.,' which have appeared in my *Notes for the Nile,* and 'XXI.,' 'XXII.,' and 'XXIII.,' which appeared in the *Academy,* these poems are printed now for the first time.

For the convenience of Nile travellers who may care to have this book with them, the poems are arranged with a view to locality rather than to subject. The traveller is supposed to see Cairo and the neighbourhood, and then pass up Nile to the First Cataract and Philae.

CONTENTS

CONTENTS

A RETURN TO EGYPT

THERE is a land where Time no count can keep,
    Where works of men imperishable seem,
    Where through Death's barren solitude doth gleam
Undying hope for them that sow and reap ;
Yea, land of life, where death is but a deep
    Warm slumber, a communicable dream,
    Where from the silent grave far voices stream
Of those that tell their secrets in their sleep.

Land of the palm-tree and the pyramid,
    Land of sweet waters from a mystic urn,
      Land of sure rest, where suns shine on for ever,
I left thee—in thy sands a heart was hid ;
      My life, my love, were cast upon thy river,
    And, lo ! to seek Osiris I return.

II

THE FIRST CALL TO PRAYER

(IN THE CITADEL COURTYARD, CAIRO, AT SUNSET)

LIKE gold, from ground to minaret,
　　Great Ali's mosque is all aglow,
　　As here we stand in silent row,
Beside the courtyard parapet.
Far pyramids to largeness grow
　　Above the vaporous plain of Nile,
　　And loftier Sultân Hasan's pile
Lifts from the Rumèleh below.

The Kaliph-tombs beyond the mounds,
　　Where stand the torn and spectral mills,
　　Are silent with a hush that stills
The neighbour city's murm'ring sounds.
With gift of glory for the hills
　　Of near Mokattam, from the west,
　　The sun is sinking to his rest,
And all the heaven with splendour fills.

THE FIRST CALL TO PRAYER

Each living thing with wonder stands
   To see rose-red the daystar's rim
   Pause on the far horizon dim,
Then plunge into the desert sands.
Hark! as with sound of seraphim
   Sudden the silent air is stirred,
   And floating far and wide, is heard
The blind Muëddin's Evening hymn.

Now high, now low, the cadence falls,
   Music of streams and summer-rhymes
   Of bees that murmur in the limes,
And far-off Alpine cattle-calls,
Seem blent with bells and silver chimes,
   In mellow mystery of sound
   That floats where mountains stand around,
From cities glad at festal times.

Sweet harmonies enchant the ear,
   And grow and surge, as man to man
   Sings resonant his loud adân,[1]
To tell the time of prayer is near.
Now fades another daylight's span,
   'God is most great,' I testify;
   'Attend unto Muhammad's cry,
Ye followers of the true Korân!'

[1] Call to prayer.

From mosque to mosque in marvellous tone
　　Clear voices rang, all else was hushed;
　　Like spray of sound the music gushed
From those tall fountain-heads of stone.
And still the heavens faintly flushed,
　　And still the message rose and fell,
　　Till over Cairo's citadel
The first star into glory rushed.

'God is most great, and there is none
　　But God, Muhammad was God-sent!
　　Come, then, to prayer and to content,
God is most great, the Only One!'
Upon the parapet we leant,
　　Our souls were called to evening prayer,
　　We felt the music in the air,
For more than Muslim hearts was meant.

NOTE.—The hours of prayer—Adân—are proclaimed by the Mueddins (or Muezzins) from the minarets of the mosques five times a day, at periods that mark the division of the Eastern day: (1) Magrib, a little after sunset; (2) Asha, nightfall, an hour and a half after sunset; (3) Subh, daybreak; (4) Duhr, midday; (5) Asr, afternoon, an hour and a half before sunset.

III

THE DANCING DERVISHES

(AT THE ĜAMÁ EL AKBAR)

THE shrillest pipe man ever played
    Was making music overhead,
And in a circle, down below,
Sat men whose faces seemed to show
Another world was all their trade.

Then up they rose, and one by one
    Shook skirts down, following him who led
To where the elder brother sat—
All gaberdine and conic hat,
Then bowed, and off for Heaven they spun.

Their hands were crossed upon the breast,
    Their eyes were closed as if in sleep,
The naked foot that beat the floor,
To keep them spinning more and more,
Was careless of all need for rest.

Soon every flowing skirt began
     Its milkwhite spinning plane to keep,
Each brother of the holy band
Spun in and out with lifted hand
A teetotum no longer man.

But I might see, how, all the while,
     With whisper low, and trembling lip,
The word of Allah's grace was given
To those that twirled from earth to Heaven,
By a stern mouth that knew no guile.

The grey old man, their leader, went
     Throughout his spinning fellowship,
And reverently to the ear,
Of every dervish circling near,
He spake a soft encouragement.

The piper piped a shriller psalm,
     The dancers thro' their mystery moved
Untouched, untouching, and the whirl
That set our giddy heads aswirl
Served but to give their faces calm.

Till very surely there was shown
     The glimpse of Paradise they loved,
Then drooped the skirts, then failed the trance,
Then one by one they left the dance,
And in the circle sat them down.

IV

EL FÂT'HA

(This prayer from the Kôrân is to the Muhammadan what
the Lord's Prayer is to the Christian.)

God of Mercy, God of Grace,
Lord of all creation's race,
To thy holy name we raise
Prayer, to thee, O God, be praise.
Prince of that dread Judgment day,
Thee we serve, to thee we pray,
Help us, lead us in thy way,
Way of those whom thou hast blest,
Upon whom no wrath shall rest,
Who from right go not astray.

AMEN.

AÎSHA'S TEARS

(OUTSIDE THE CITY WALLS)

AÎSHA[1] sobs as one in pain,
With dates and palm-branch in her hand,
Goes thro' the city-gates alone
To weep for him, her husband, gone
Into the far-off silent land
Not ever to return again.

How changed from when on funeral-day,
Thro' dark bazaar and alley dim,
The young boy-reader went before,
And cried to Allah bending o'er
His prophet, to bend over him,
And scattered scent along the way.

For then, on turbaned heads borne high,
The coffin in procession went
Almost in triumph, and the blind
Led the death-blinded, and behind
Was ululation and lament,
And prayers from many a passer-by.

---

[1] Aîsha should be pronounced as if it were written 'ay-ee-sha.'

Then in the grave they laid him, head
Towards Mecca, and the master came
And taught the dumb man what to say
When heralds of the Judgment Day—
The dreadful angels none may name—
Came inquisitioning the dead—

Why doth Aisha shed the tear?
The days of weeping sure should end—
This is the fortieth day since then;
She lost no lover among men
When Ali died, she gained a friend—
Freedom from one whose word was fear.

Her funeral feasts have all been made,
Her chamber walls are dark of hue,
Her mats were turned the other side,
The day her lord and master died,
Her hands are still deep-stained with blue,
Her hair is still without its braid;

And when they bore, as she doth know,
His body to the mosque, and cried
Above it prayers from the Korân,
All present vowed he was a man,
Pious and good and justified;
Then wherefore should her tears still flow?

Poor girl!   She feels there is a God
Who looks upon the heart, and well
She knows that, when those angels dread
Come close to catechise the dead,
They 'll beat his body down to hell
Seven times, with flail of iron rod.

And though within the grave's dark room
The five replies were duly given,—
' God, one God,' ' True, Muhammad's word,'
' The Kââba, Kibleh,' ' Allah, Lord,'
' Islam the Faith,'—with heads of seven
The snakes will sting him until Doom.

NOTE.—The Muhammadans believe that, on the night following
the burial of the dead, the two angels, Munkar and Nakir, with long
hair and glowing eyes, terrible teeth, and bearing iron flails in their
hands, will visit the tomb, and catechise the dead as to the five
articles of faith required of all true followers of the Prophet.

If approved, the soul, which is lingering with the body to await
this preliminary trial, is allowed a foretaste of Paradise—otherwise,
the body of the dead man is beaten down into hell with iron rods,
and, seven times rejected, undergoes this torment seven times, as a
preliminary taste of the eternal pain in store for him.

Ninety-nine serpents, with seven heads, called ' Tannin,' are then
sent into his sepulchre.   It is the office of these serpents to sting and
bite, and blow up the bodies of the wicked until the Day of Judg-
ment.

VI

STREET CRIES

(IN CAIRO)

' YA semeet, yâ, yâ semeet,'
Shrill it echoes down the street,
Buy a cake, O merchant, eat !

' Oranges, O gentleman !
Sweet as honey ever ran
Are the Benha burtukan.' [1]

' Here is sugar for a nail,
Iron scraps I seek by sale,
Halâwee will never fail.'

' Taste my green pistachios,
From the prophet's blood, God knows,
Bloomed the thorn into a rose.'

' Ya effendi, you may smile,
But my lupins they beguile,—
Little children of the Nile ! '

[1] The Yusef Effendi oranges—'burtukan'—from Benha, are much prized in the Cairene market.

'Roasted pips! Abdalláwee!
Taste my melon-pips, and ye
Never shall in trouble be.'

'Scent from Paradise in showers!
Maidens, fit for bridal bowers,
Here are fragrant henna flowers!'

'God will make my lemons light,
Allah send me sup and bite,
Legs, O Kadi! Left and Right!'

So I hear above the din,
Of the Sûk-en-Nahhâsîn,
Words that honest bread would win.

But where all is noise and heat,
In the Muski's motley street,
Cups that clink, with prayer entreat

Saying, 'Think, ye thirsty, think
Of the hand whose cup I clink,
Him whose bounty gives ye drink.'

And in thought as on I stroll,
Grateful for the water's dole,
What if Heaven should touch my soul?

So that with his leathern can,
When the greasy-goat-skin man
Butt against my body ran,

I must, to his heart's surprise,
Give a 'kirsh' [1] to him who cries
' My poor pay is Paradise.' [2]

[1] Small silver coin, value $2\frac{1}{2}$d.

[2] The water-bearers or 'Sakka' men in Cairo have hard work and very small pay; this fact they emphasise by their street cries : 'Ya auwad Allah,' 'God will reward me.'

VII

THE FATHER OF THE CATS

BARE to the waist, and wild of locks,
  The Dervish on his camel sways,
And back and forward as he rocks
  Above the town's tumultuous ways,
He bears the cry by wall and dome,
' The Father of the Cats has come ! '

The Father of the Cats, he smiles,
  And from his camel-bag he takes
A puss he nursed a thousand miles,
  And o'er the laughing crowd he shakes
His furry charge, while at his breast
Another purrs to be caressed.

Another and another peeps
  From out the ' houritch,' [1] just for fun,
Cat-father prodigal he keeps
  Full fifty daughters of the sun,
Who over desert sands have gone
To see the black Kååba stone.

[1] Camel-bag.

The camel, with high nose in air,
   Stalks proudly thro' the city's pack,
As if he felt almost aware
   That goddesses were on his back,
As if he bore as on he pass't
Astarte, Aphrodite, Bast.

No more to fair Bubastis' shrine
   With pipe and song the votaries seek,
We drink to-day a poorer wine,
   The prophet's cup at Zagazeek ;
But still the Meccan pilgrim knows
Men pay the Cat-head goddess vows.

And these poor tabbies, as of old,
   Are emblems of the powers that are ;
The 'hadj,'[1] in tempest, heat and cold,
   Feels Passion, sun, and Love, his star,
And dreams the narrow pathway lies
Thro' passionate love to Paradise.

But what, O Father of the Cats,
   Are symbols to a hungry man ?
Better to know no mice or rats
   Will plague your pilgrim's caravan,
That meal in camel-bags will stay,
If ' Pasht ' be guardian of your way.

      [1] Pilgrim to Mecca.

NOTE.—It is perhaps a relic of the worship of Pasht or Bast at Bubastis, of which Herodotus gives us so glowing an account, that still each year, with the Caravan to Mecca, there goes a camel laden with cats, in the care of an old Dervish who is generally known as the 'Father of the Cats.'

It is doubtless also with an eye to the preservation of the Caravan from a plague of rats and mice during their halts that poor puss is thus compelled to be an annual pilgrim. The goddess Pasht or Sekhet Bast was a daughter of the Sun, who warred continually against the demon of the night.

VIII

DESERTED BY THE CARAVAN

'God! He is one God!' so I testify,
  'Muhammad His apostle, he alone!'
I, ready in this wilderness to die
  Forsaken and fordone!

I scarce had thought when I my turban wound,
  With its long yards of gauzy cotton-cloud,
That of my head's uncovering would be found
  So soon my body's shroud.[1]

I little dreamed, when first our pilgrim-band
  Went forth with boom of cannon, strong and brave,
That for these weary limbs my fainting hand
  Would scoop a desert-grave.

Yet, tho' my tongue unto my mouth doth cleave,
  And tho' my last ablution be of dust
For lack of sprinkled water—I believe,
  In Allah is my trust.

---

[1] The orthodox length of a believer's turban is equal to the length of his body, in order that it may be used as the wearer's winding-sheet.

For I have seen the strange light in the sky
  That leaps, unwavering, o'er the Prophet's tomb ;
Have known the secrets of our faith, that lie
  Hid in the Kââba's womb ;

Have wandered round the cloistered colonnade
  Of El Medineh only pilgrims know ;
Have climbed the Holy Hill, and duly paid
  My sacrificial vow.

Wherefore, forsaken of the Caravan,
  No hope of tears no mourners to attend,
The vultures' wings above, a dying man,
  I still can call Death friend.

For what is Life but pilgrimage, and Death
  The one sure rest for feet too tired to live ;
To God the Pitiful, Who gave me breath,
  My breath again I give.

Self-shrouded, in his self-made grave he lay,
  A strong wind rose and covered him with sand ;
No weary pilgrim gladlier passed away
  Into the Peaceful Land.

IX

THE SAKÎYEH AT THE FOUNTAIN OF THE SUN

(AIN SHEMS)

ROUGH clout upon his patient head,
   The stately camel round doth go,
With gentle, hesitating tread;
And yoked, and blind with frontlets, made
   Of black Nile-mud, the buffalo
Plies with him his unequal trade.

There, on the shaft, the father sits,
   And with him perch his children four,
Chewing the sugar-cane to bits;
No touch of goad, no lift of hand,
   And still the streaming vases pour
Then dive upon the endless band.

And so, from rise to set of sun
   Unintermittent for a space,
From forth the well the waters run—
Sweet waters that the Virgin knew,
   When Jesus rested in this place—
The waters that the Sun-priests drew.

'Old fountain of the sun,' I cried,
  'The priests, whom Moses met at An,
Have passed, and great Usert'sen's pride
Has vanished, save for one tall stone;
  But still your service unto man,
With love, unceasingly is done.

Tho' here no more the Bennu[1] bird
  May bring his ash, and drink his fill,
The ground to resurrection stirred
Is instinct with the power of spring,
  And knows it is of Heaven's good-will
That life from death its gift should bring.

And these poor yoke-fellows, that make
  Sweet bounty by the wheel that burrs
From morn till evening-time, will take
Rich blessing from the hearts that feel,
  That all the true Sun-worshippers
Must bow to the Sakiyeh wheel.'

---

[1] The Bennu bird, Palm bird, or Phœnix, sacred to Ra, was said to raise itself to life at the end of every 500 years and to return to Heliopolis, where it was worshipped, bringing its ashes with it.

X

AT HELIOPOLIS

STERN lifts the lonely pillar o'er the mounds
    Usert'sen set before the Halls of Tum,
One time it heard the loud Sun-worship sounds,
    It only hears to-day the wild bees hum.

Where sacred lions roared above their prey,
    And glad the votaries fed the milk-white sow,
Where the bull Mnevis bellowed to the day
    Is waste and silent melancholy now.

But thou art eloquent, thou mighty stone,
    Albeit the bees have blurred thy written sign;
Firm on thy red imperishable throne
    Thou tellest still of other days than mine.

For Abram saw thee, fearing for his wife,
    Thee Joseph gazed on when he ruled the land;
Thou didst o'erlook the patriot at his strife,
    Thou knewest well what Moses hid in sand.

To thee the Sun-priest's daughter paid her vow
    When first that Hebrew, saved from out the flood,
Skilled in all wisdom the Egyptians know,
    Learned how the flame of love can fire the blood.

Thee Plato, musing in the fields of An,
    Eudoxus, Strabo with the searching eyes
Honoured, and here, the wise Ionian
    Talked of the gods and learned their histories.

Led by thy golden-headed glory bright,[1]
    Pianchi with his bulls and balsam came;
Great Alexander, resting from his fight,
    Knew thee unhurt by fierce Cambyses' flame.

How should fire touch thee, pillar without peers!
    To thee the 'Bennu' bird from isles of palm
Eight times at end of her five hundred years
    Has brought her ash and found thee strong and calm.

Nor only here the risen bird of Ra
    Gave hope for rising to the child of On,
Here rose in later times our Morning Star,
    The Virgin Mother hither bore her Son.

The whole wide world has rolled to light from shade
    Since first thy shadow lengthened with the day,
But Love's new morning is but newly made,
    Stand till high noon has cast all shade away.

---

[1] The top of the obelisk was coated with 'Smu' metal, probably burnished copper, till a comparatively recent date.

XI

THE OBELISK AT HELIOPOLIS

(SET UP BEFORE THE TEMPLE OF TUM BY USERTESEN I.
ABOUT B.C. 2443)

HE who set this stone where it stands
    Was 'Hor of the Sun,' the Life for men,
King of the Upper and Lower lands,
    Cheper-ka-ra Usertesen.

He, the Lord of the double crown,
    Life for all that of woman is born—
Usertesen, long let his name be known,
    Son of the Sun-god Ra—the morn.

Friend of all the spirits of On,
    Golden Hor in his loved abode,
Life of the father and life of the son,
    Cheper-ka-ra, beneficent God.

He it was planted this stone whence it rears
    Full in front of the Sun-god's portal,
Gave it the feast of the thirty years,
    He the Dispenser of Life Immortal.

So from the midst of the silent heaps,
The broken walls of the city of An,
Speaks the pillar that solemnly keeps
The faith of a god, the trust of a man.

NOTE.—The translation of the hieroglyphics inscribed upon the obelisk of Heliopolis, which is embodied in the above poem, is taken from Brugsch's *Egypt under the Pharaohs*, vol. i. chap. ix. p. 131.

XII

MENA HOUSE

THIS was 'The Way of the gods' of old,
  Full of magic and mystery then,[1]
    This is 'The Way of the gods' to-day—
Gods whose authority comes of gold,
  French, Americans, Englishmen,
    Gods who rule as far as they pay.

By the side of the road from over the Nile
  The long wire hums, and away in the town
    Men speak and whisper across the plain;
And under the Lebbeks for many a mile
  The coach rattles on, and the horn is blown,
    And the red-coated driver handles the rein.

And here at the end of the high-banked road
  In 'the land of the gods,' where the dead men are,
    As white as milk thro' the avenue seen
Is a place of pleasure, the gods' abode;
  You can hear the twangle of lute and guitar,
    You can see the gods at the balcony lean.

---

[1] 'The Way of the gods,' or 'the Holy Road,' which ran from the west of the Heliopolitan nome, by old Babylon, across the plain to the Pyramids, was looked upon as full of mystery and haunted.

And out on the daïs beneath the shade,
 With talk and tea to their heart's desire,
  They watch the players of tennis run ;
And the scarab-barterer plies his trade,
 The gay-tasselled camel comes for hire,
  The ass and his driver wait in the sun.

But when the dark on the desert falls,
 When the last rogue-villager hies him home,
  And the stars o'er the Pyramid twinkle bright,
The gods sit at ease in their Arab-halls
 And feast, while music throbs in the dome,
  'Neath starry clusters of magical light.

Then careless they, tho' they jest above
 The graves where old Egypt came with a sigh
  With beating of breasts and clapping of hands,
The gods and goddesses laugh and love
 With never a thought of the death-hour nigh,
  And thread the dance in their rhythmic bands.

XIII

THE PYRAMID OF MEN-KAU-RA

WHEN old Ptah-hotep took his stand
  In that Red Temple, at the Feast,
And lifted up his guardian hand
  Beside the lotus-bearing priest.

He knew accursèd was the sleep
  Of him who reared 'Chut's' pyramid,[1]
That under 'Ur's' gigantic heap [2]
  A tyrant of mankind was hid.

But this good ruler's heart of trust,
  Who piled the Ethiopian stone
Above his sleeping-place, was just,
  He thought with love on him alone.

And often as he walked around
  To see none harmed the royal tomb,
From out the granite slope would sound
  Words from the coffin in its womb.

[1] Chut was the ancient name of the Great Pyramid, built by Chufu or Cheops, B.C. 3733.

[2] Ur was the ancient name of the second pyramid, built by Chephren, B.C. 3666.

'Osiris, king of South and North,
    Men-kau-ra, evermore to live,
The heaven of heavens brought thee forth,
    The sky and earth thy life did give.

Thy mother Nut, above thee spread,
    Wraps thee in mystery divine,
In grace lifts up thy royal head
    And sets thee with the gods to shine.

And now thou art where peace is sure,
    No foes thy kingly sleep distress,
Men-kau-ra ever to endure
    In everlasting happiness.'

For he who levelled here the ground,
    And piled the granite line on line,
He knew that law alone was sound
    Which had its root in things divine.

He flung the temple-buildings wide,
    He set the serf from bondage free,
He heard the poor man when he cried,
    And justice did, with love, decree.

Ptah-hotep from the temple went,
    'Longer,' he cried, 'than mounded stone
Good deeds shall be the monument
    Of Men-kau-ra, the living one.

Tho' hands of greed one day may break
    The granite portals of his sleep,
Tho' robbers over seas shall take
    And plunge his coffin in the deep.

Tho' time may level with the sand
    His tomb divine beside the river,
Men-kau-ra's monument shall stand,
    His righteousness shall live for ever.'

NOTES.—The inscription on the fragments of Men-kau-ra's coffin, now in the British Museum, reads: ' Osiris, king of the North and South, Men-kau-ra, living for ever, the heavens have produced thee; thou wast engendered by Nut (the sky), thou art the offspring of Seb (the earth). Thy mother Nut spreads over thee in her form as a divine mystery. She has granted thee to be a god; thou shalt never more have enemies, O king of the North and South, Men-kau-ra, living for ever.'

Ptah-hotep, whose tomb is at Sakkarah, was a priest of the Pyramids of Asa, Ra-en-user, and the ' Divine dwelling of Men-kau-hor,' and lived in the fifth dynasty.

Readers of Herodotus, Book II., 129, 134, will remember the good character, given by the historian, of Mycerinus, builder of the third pyramid, B.C. 3633. An attempt was made to destroy this pyramid in A.D. 1196. Howard Vyse discovered the sarcophagus of the king *in situ* in 1837. It was lost in the Bay of Biscay by shipwreck, and only an inscribed portion of the wooden coffin which floated was saved.

XIV

MORNING MIST ON THE GREAT PYRAMID

I CLIMBED great Chufu's giant stair,
    I felt the anguish of the stones,
Loud lamentation filled the air,
    And cries of vengeance against thrones.

From Abu-rôash' northern height,
    Far south to ancient Abu-sir,
Its shadow seemed to surge thro' light,
    Its sorrow still was in mine ear.

The massive doors I entered in,
    Before, and up the gallery-slope
There went a tyrant's pride and sin,
    A people's toil that had no hope.

Upon its mighty head I stood,
    The scene was fair, as fair could be;
There Paradise and fruitful flood,
    And here the desert's barren sea.

But from the quarry, choked with sands,
   Came sounds of agony and woe,
Men toiled like cattle, driven in bands;
   I heard the curse and frequent blow.

From burning cliffs on yonder shore,
   Thro' mid-day sun and sweltering haze,
Laborious rafts their burdens bore,
   To drop them at the landing-ways.

I said, 'Has time no power to hide
   The shame of this gigantic pile?
Must still its horror, far and wide,
   Be cast upon the land of Nile?

Is there no Khalif[1] who will dare
   To grapple with these terrace-stones,
To pluck this giant's body bare,
   And build a city with its bones?

That so no more, above the plain,
   Above the desert's rolling waves,
Shall loom this monument of pain,
   This dread memorial-tomb to slaves.

[1] A reference to Melik-el-Kamil, who, at the beginning of the thirteenth century, made an attempt to destroy one of the Pyramids, but, after months of toil, only succeeded in stripping off the covering of one of the sides.

The sun sank down, the shadow grew,
   But still the mountain was not hid;
The night its curtain overdrew,
   But could not veil the Pyramid.

And darkening all the world below,
   Where the dead men unnumbered are,
Rose up its mass moon-white as snow
   To blur the heavens and blot the star.

But when the Sphinx, with wondering face,
   Flushed faintly to another morn,
And, springing in a moment's space
   From earth to heaven, the day was born,

The sun, that mounted o'er the plain,
   Wove from the dew a fleecy shroud,
And wrapped the pyramid of pain
   From mortal sight in mystic cloud.

XV

THE DREAM OF THOTHMES IV

THERE is no need, great Hormachu,[1] for thee
To open lips and speak to kings in dream,
For now thy limbs from desert-sand are free,
And to thy temple, down the steps can stream
The men who come to wonder or to pray.

But here in 'Roset,'[2] at the ancient gate
Of the dim under-world, where dead men are,
I, lying at the noon, was dreaming late
Of those past days when Thothmes drove his car
Keen in his lion-quest on hunting-day.

And since upon his tablet plain is graved
The old-world tale of how the hunter-king
Heard the Sphinx speak, when of his hand it craved
Deliverance from the sand's long covering,
To tell it to the new world I essay.

---

[1] Hormachu—the Harmachis of the Greeks—was one of the names of the Sphinx, = ' Horus in the Horizon,' probably the Sun at Midday.

[2] In Thothmes' time the burial-ground round the Pyramids, already abandoned, was spoken of as Roset = ' Door to the under-world.'

Here of old Prince Thothmes came, so the granite
    tablet tells,
The Prince whom the Sphinx made a king,
On his lordly pastime bent,
Cast the spear at the ring,
Bolts at brazen target sent,
And to hunt the lion went
With his chariot and two horses in the 'valley of
    gazelles.'

At the hour of high noon, when he gave his servants
    rest,
Unto Hormachu he brought,
In the city of the dead,
Offering fair of mountain flowers,
And with prayer the goddess sought
Who of Memphis-town is head,
She whose bosom Horus fed,
And with vows he came to call
On Her who guards the towers
Of the north and southern wall,[1]
And on Sekhet feared at Zois,
And on Set and Rannu blest.

Now of all the places none is so weird as the abode
Of great Khepra, where the road[2]

---

[1] Isis.   [2] See note, p. 25.

Of the gods, so full of fear,
From of old doth eastward run,
From the setting of the sun
O'er the plain, and goeth straight
Unto On, from very near
The Sphinx, whose monument
Doth Khepra represent—
Of spirits the most great :—
The Sphinx, whose ruddy face
Shines forth with Khepra's grace,
Khepra, he who in this place
Doth remain a mighty god.

Thothmes came unto the place, left his car, and
    wandered on.
He was weary, wanted rest,
And himself adown he laid
In the great god's mighty shade,
And sleep sank into his breast,
And a wondrous dream he dreamed.
It was noontide, and it seemed
That the god's own mouth spake words as a father to
    a son.

'Behold me, my son Thothmes, I am Hormachu thy sire,
I am Khepra, Ra, and Tum,[1]

---

[1] The Sun of the Midnight, the Sun in the East, the Sun in the
West, under which forms Hormachu the Sphinx was worshipped.

Unto thee this land shall come
And the kingship; thou shalt wear
The white crown, and the red
Shall be placed upon thy head,
Thou, young Seb, the earth-god's heir;
And the earth it shall be thine
Far as his great eyes do shine
Who is lord of all the lands.
Plenty, riches thine shall be,
Borne by furthest people's hands,
From the north and southern nation
Shall full tribute come to thee,
And of years a long duration
Shall be granted, for my face
Smiles upon thee with its grace,
And my heart to thee it clings.
With the best of all earth's things,
Thothmes' son, on one condition, to enrich thee I
    .   desire.

Think of me as thy peculiar flesh, of bone thy very
    bone.
Lo, the sand how it doth cover,
Blown by centuries of storm,
How encroaching it wraps over
All my moveless, godlike form !
Do the wish within my heart,

Yea, unwrap these wreaths of sand,
So shall all men understand
That to me a son thou art;
Come thou near me, let me be
As a Father unto thee,
Lo! I take thee by the hand, Thothmes, thou and I
    are one.'

Then Thothmes he awoke at the ending of these
    words,
And he recognised the sign,
Felt the message was divine,
And made silence very deep
In his heart these words to keep.
' Let us go,' said he, 'and bring
To the Sphinx uncovering,
For the honour of the king
Khafra good, and for the sake
Of the image he dared make
Unto Harmachis and Tum,
That again the folk may come
Here with prayer and offering.'

So they dug away the sands,
Bared the Temple where it stands
In the Sphinx's mighty hands;
Egypt's priests and people all,

When young Thothmes wore the red

And white crown upon his head,

Came again to festival;

Geese in thousands, beer and bread,

Wine and oil and incense brought

To the God whom Khafra wrought,

Great guardian, Lord of Lords,

Where to-day a granite tablet the royal dream
    records.

NOTE.—The translation of the dream of Thothmes IV., upon which this poem is based, was made by S. Birch—*Records of the Past*, vol. xii. p. 143. But I have availed myself also of the fuller translation given by M. Brugsch, in his *Egypt under the Pharaohs*, vol. i. p. 415. The inscription from which these translations are made is found upon a granite tablet, about 14 feet high, placed before the breast of the great Sphinx at Gîzeh. Travellers to Egypt should not leave the Pyramids without a careful examination of this remarkable dream-tablet, set up in the month Athyr, and on the nineteenth day, in the year 1 of Thothmes IV., B.C. 1533.

XVI

BEFORE THE STATUE OF CHEPHREN

(GÎZEH MUSEUM)

How many months did, unrewarded, ring
 The chisels on this adamantine stone,
 Before the grey-green diorite would own
The right of man from out its heart to bring
Such royal form, the hawk with outstretched wing,
 The rush and lily, linked upon the throne,
 Before, between the lion-heads was known
The lord whom men saluted, god and king!

There Chephren sits, and there shall sit for aye,
 With wide contemptuous unregardful eyes
  That saw the people's pain, and were unmoved;
  That watched the great tomb-monument he loved
 Grow like a mountain in the western skies,
But knew that Death could never end his day.

XVII

SISTE VIATOR, ORA PRO NOBIS!

ENTEF sits in solemn rest,
See one hand is on his breast,
One outstretched with joy to take
Bowl of wine and flesh and cake:
Underneath his master's chair
Waits the hound; and cool the air
Blows about him from the fan
Of the grave fly-flapper man.

Entef cannot speak or think
Till his soul have meat and drink.
Bring him food, and pray the gods
Speed it through their drear abodes,
So that Entef in Amenti,
Finding fruit and flesh in plenty,
May remember what was done
When he dwelt beneath the Sun;
See again his pleasant fields,
Know what wine his vintage yields,
Count his labourers, tell his flocks,
Drive his asses, slay the ox;

Laugh at dance and tumblers gay,
Hear the old blind harper play,
Watch the sword-stick flash and crack,
Wrestlers straining arm and back,
Know again the sportsman's zest,
Feel again his knees caressed
By the children and the wife
Whom he loved as he loved life.

Stranger, let the words be read
Over Entef's princely head;
They are words will give him rest,
The reciter shall be blest.

'Ye who live upon the earth,
Simply born, of gentle birth,
Priest or scribe or minister,
Yea, or layman, entering here
To this tomb with bated breath,
Loving life and hating death,
Wishing from the city's gods
Favour for your own abodes,
Fleeing from the wrath to come,
And in your eternal home
Praying that your rest may be
Endless in security,
Hoping to your children's hands
To transmit your name and lands—

You, if scribe you are, recite
Words that on this stone I write,
Or if words you cannot spell,
Hear them read, repeat them well.

Saying " Offerings be thine,
Amen, lord of Karnak's shrine,
That he of his grace will give
So that Entef's soul may live,
Thousands of the loaves we bake,
Thousands of the wine we make,
Thousands of fat oxen bred,
Thousands of the geese well-fed,
Thousands too of garments meet
For the soul in his retreat.
So that all things pure and good
For his living shadowhood
May be his who bids you pray,
Ere you pass upon your way." '

NOTE.—The funerary inscription, of which this is a metrical
rendering, is translated by M. Maspero, 'Conference,' p. 382.

M. de Rouget dates it as belonging to the twelfth dynasty. A
similar invocation is seen at the tomb of Ameni Amenemhat, at Beni
Hassan.   Travellers will remember the famous Stele of Entef in the
Gîzeh Museum, which is described in the first part of the poem.

The Egyptians believed that the shadow, or Ka, or double, of the
deceased could not be fully alive in the next world unless an
abundance of food was supplied it by way of offerings brought to the
tomb-chamber on stated days.

XVIII

THE SHÊKH EL BELED

(IN THE GÎZEH MUSEUM)

HE stands as village shêkh he stood
    Five thousand years gone by,
A creature of acacia wood
    Too living far to die.

He holds his ruler's staff in hand;
    And seems as bluff and bold
As when he overlooked his land
    In Memphian days of old.

His bullet head, his close-kept ear,
    Strong lip and double chin,
Those stony eyes so full of fear
    For idleness and sin.

Ah! Shêkh el Beled, who would shirk
    If such a presence now
Came forth to oversee the work
    And watch the plowmen plow?

You lived in days when there were twain
    Alone beneath the sun,
The man who toiled and tilled the plain,
    The man who saw it done.

And yet one other thing it seems
    Grew fat beside the Nile—
Humour, for lo ! your kind face beams
    And broadens into smile.

XIX

THE LADY NEFERT

(IN THE GÎZEH MUSEUM)

LADY of liquid eyes and skin more fair
    Than that dear 'favourite of the Sun,' your lord,
    Who one time wooed you with a lover's word,
And bound the daisy fillet in your hair;
You saw Seneferu's pyramid, stair on stair,
    Rise snowy white, you heard with one accord
    The wail of ancient Egypt when they stored,
Within, his bones who made 'the Good' his care.

You little thought that from his mountainous tomb
    The King should cease, but you his prince's wife,
        Unharmed for full five thousand years would rest,
From out the dark sand's tutelary womb
        To bring the truth your faithful lips attest,
That Love's great good is happy wedded life.

Close by the Mêdûm Pyramid, built by the last king of the third
dynasty, Seneferu, whose name is said to mean 'maker of the
good,' there was discovered in 1872, by Mariette Bey, what are
probably the oldest portrait-statues in the world. Visitors to the
Gîzeh Museum will remember well the life-like expression, calm

dignity of their faces, their marvellously fresh colouring, and their glistening eyes.   These are the limestone statues of Ra Hotep, son of Seneferu, high priest of On, and commander of the king's warriors, and his wife the lady Nefert.   They are seated side by side, Ra Hotep (favourite of the sun-god Ra) is of darker complexion, and sits bare to the waist, holding a roll of papyrus in his left hand to show that he is a man of education.   Nefert, the beautiful, with fillet of riband starred with daisies in her hair, and with a banded necklet of pear-shaped jewels round her neck, is fairer of skin, and sits with folded. hands, clad in a white garment close fitting above the breast.   The eyes of both of these statues have a peculiar lustre, owing to the fact that behind the crystal of which they are composed, is a thin plate of silver to give light and life to them.

XX

A QUEEN'S GAZELLE

(IN THE GÎZEH MUSEUM)

MIGHTY mother of Priest-kings, say
　　How fares it now in the ' Fields of the Sun,'
Does the little gazelle of your earthly play
　　To the voice of your calling run?

You are sleeping still in your painted chest,
　　The funeral meats at your side are laid,
Three thousand years you have taken your rest,
　　And still your soul is a shade ! [1]

But the hearts of us mortals are yet the same,
　　Still, still we can honour the gentle Queen,
She whose voice by its charm could tame
　　The timidest thing that had been.

---

[1] At the end of the three thousand years it was believed the soul would re-enter the body, and the dead would arise.

She who could call her gazelle so fond
    Back from its haunts in the Theban hill,
She who believed in a life beyond
    For creatures we care but to kill.

She who dying could think of the dead
    —Her playmate wrapped in its linen rolls,
And pray it might lie at her feet, or her head,
    For joy in the land of souls.

Uast-Em-Khebit, the broiderers bent,
    Not without tears, o'er their task that morn ;
They stitched at the glorious funeral tent
    Whereunder your body was borne.

When the patch-work squares into beauty grew,
    And the hawk of the sun shone out like fire,
They thought of your soul as a hawk that flew,
    They remembered your soul's desire.

And there on the curtain, your sleep above,
    They wrought, 'mid the clusters of palm, the
        gazelle,
And about its neck, for a garland, wove
    The lilies you loved so well.

NOTE.—In the coffin of Uast-Em-Khebit, mother of Pinotem III., last of the Priest-King dynasty of the Her-Hor line (twenty-first dynasty, 1100-1000 B.C.), were found not only the mummied funeral meats, but a very carefully embalmed gazelle, in a coffin shaped to its body's form.

The funeral tent of this Queen was also discovered, close by the coffin, in the great Deir el Bahari Royal-mummy find, 1881. It is of leathern patch-work, of squares of various colour. Amongst the ornaments of this funeral canopy or tent may be seen stars, daisies, scarabs, uraeus-disk basilisks, and a great hawk of gold; while on the frieze have been wrought, by way of ornament, gazelles crouching by palm clusters, having lotus garlands round their necks.

This unique and interesting object is after careful restoration pre-served in the Gîzeh Museum, where also may be seen the mummied gazelle of the Egyptian Queen.

XXI

THE MUMMY OF SESOSTRIS

(WITH M. MASPERO IN THE BOULAK MUSEUM, CAIRO,
JUNE IST, 1886)

AMONG his perfumed wrappings Ramses lay,
    Son of the Sun, the conqueror without peers ;
    The jewel-holes were in his wounded ears,
His lips tight-closed above th' embalmer's clay ;
Unguent had turned his white locks amber-grey,
    And on his puissant chin fresh from the shears
    The thin hair gleamed which full three thousand
        years
Of careless sleep could never disarray.

Hands henna-stained across his ample breast
    Were laid in peace ; but though the warrior's eyes
    Flamed fire no more beneath the forward brow,
His keen hawk-nose such pride, such power expressed,
    Near Kadesh stream we heard the Hittite cries,
    And saw by Hebrew toil San's temple-cities grow.

XXII

AN OLD-WORLD HERO

(THE UNWRAPPING OF TÁÁ-KEN, BOULAK MUSEUM,
JUNE 9, 1886, BY M. E. GRÉBAUT)

WHEN that dark face beneath the triple blow
    Lay battered, tongue bit thro', and mouth awry,
    And o'er Táá-Ken's last death agony
The Theban warriors felt their freedom grow,
They little thought far centuries would know
    Those cruel wounds had never ceased to cry,
    Till Egypt broke the Hyksos tyranny,
And great Avaris 'mid her reeds was low.

Fierce axe might answer thus that brave word sent,
    'Servant I am, yet serve what God I will!'
      But seed of independence then was sown
      In blood that rained from thrust of lance and bill!
      And lo! the rightful Pharaoh on his throne!
And Shepherd-Kings in lasting banishment!

NOTE.—Ra-Sekenen, or Táá-Ken, = Táá, the Brave, was a
Theban prince of the seventeenth dynasty, who, when peremptorily
ordered by the Shepherd-King Apepi to reject the worship of Amon
Ra in favour of the Hyksos god of the Delta, Set or Suteck,
stoutly refused, and headed the revolt that eventually drove the
Hyksos from Egypt, B.C. 1700. He fell in battle of terrible wounds
that may be seen upon his forehead to-day.

XXIII

AFTER THE BATTLE OF MAHUTA

SON of the Sun, Ra-amses, lord of war,
  When from the North he drave his Syrian bride
  With peace, the Hebrews in the clay-pits cried,
' Our treasure city is too mean by far
For such a King ! '—The basilisk like a star
  Burned at his forehead, his great heart to guide
  He held the Cross of Life; and at his side
The lion ramped, grim footman of his car.

Oh ! had they seen but yesterday the strife
  That choked Bubastis' channel, and the dead
    Plaguing its stream with loathsomeness ; or heard
    The Christian cannon speak its dreadful word
  Above Mahuta's waste, they ne'er had said,
' Praised be the Lion-lord who bears the Cross of Life ! '

XXIV

IN THE FIELDS OF MÎT-RAHÎNEH

WHEN I remember of that pleasant place
   Which God gave unto Adam for to keep,
   And how He took His Moses from the sheep,
And from the plough-tail to the chiefest place
Raised up a chosen prophet; when I trace
     Plain on the tombs that guard old Egypt's sleep
     How princes went to watch their servants reap,
And kingly farmers ruled a farmer's race,

Then do I think it is a royal thing
   To work with sun and water on the land,
     To labour in the fields till eventide;
     For he who toils finds God is at his side;
He feels the Almighty's hand within his hand,
And, crowned with patience, of his fate is king.

XXV

LIFTING THE COLOSSAL STATUE OF RAMESES II

(NEAR MÎT-RAHÎNEH)

WHEN with the breath of fire upon his face,
  And scarce escaped Pelusium's treachery,
To Ptah the king his statues twain would place,
  He thought not here to lie
A bruisèd hulk, to cover up whose shame
Each year the Nile with strong compassion came.

Did something of the sorrow of a king
  Cast down, dishonoured, enter heart of stone,
That, when we strove to raise the battered thing
  And set him on his throne,
Face downward still, for all our wish to save—
Our oaken beams and ram—he sank into his grave?

But slow and sure against his royal will,
  Moved by the lever's pulses fiercely plied,
The giant statue yielded to our skill,
  We turned him on his side,
And saw, upon his belt and on his hand,
The words our day can dimly understand.

'First favourite of the Sun, Light, Strength and Truth,
  Ramses, beloved of Ammon,' so we read
The royal titles that the Memphian youth
  Spake low, and bowed the head.
The sun shines still, Truth stands, and God's light grows,
But power has passed from off these marble brows.

NOTE.—The statue of Rameses II., which now lies face upward above the ground, under the care of an Arab guardian, by the side of the road that runs from Bedrashên to Mît-Rahîneh, is one of the two colossal limestone statues which were placed in front of the Bull arena, or, as some say, in front of the Temple of Ptah or Vulcan, at Memphis, by Rameses II., to commemorate his escape from death by fire after a banquet which his treacherous brother gave at Pelusium. This statue was discovered by Caviglia and Sloane in 1820, and was presented to the British Museum.

It used to lie face downward in a great ditch, and was covered by Nile inundation for part of every year. During the winter of 1886-7 Gen. Stevenson raised a subscription with a view to lifting it out of its grave and turning it face upward; he intrusted this difficult task to Major Arthur Bagnold, R.E., who borrowed a couple of 600-ton water rams and jacks from the Fleet, and having first of all placed beneath the monster a solid staging of oaken beams, set the hydraulic rams to work, and by means of careful wedging lifted it inch by inch. It was my good fortune to be passing the place at the very moment when the rams were set to work, and Major Bagnold did me the honour of asking me to take a turn at the pumps first. The only effect produced was, that the rams, by their resistance, made the whole platform of oaken beams beneath the statue sink deeper into the ground. It was some time before a solid bottom was reached and the raising of the statue could begin. As a portrait-statue of the great Pharaoh, it is one of the most noteworthy in Egypt.

XXVI

AT THE TOMB OF THI

FIFTH DYNASTY, CIRCA 3500 B.C.

(SAKKARAH)

Down thro' the trough of sliding sand
  We pass to that twelve-pillared hall,
    Where one time met the friends of Thi.
We bring no present in our hand
  Save rev'rent love to read the wall,
    And wonder for the days gone by.

No offering-slab is laid before
  The incense-chink of the recess,
    Where once the statue, painted stone,
Stood for five thousand years and more,
  To take a blessing and to bless—
    The place is empty, Thi is gone.

But we have seen him where he stands
  At Gîzeh,—apron starched with pride,
    His left foot forward as he went
Close-wigged to view the Temple lands,
  His arms down-hanging at his side,
    His face keen-eyed and eloquent.

Still privy-councillor of the King
  Beside the portal, pictured great,
    He leans upon his staff of might.
Gazelle o'er neck, and goose by wing
  The servants bear him; each estate
    Sends baskets-full of all delight.

Slave maidens dutiful and fair,
  With jewels on each swelling breast,
    Clad in soft raiment that unveils
But half conceals their beauty, bear
  For Thi the food he loved the best—
    The fowl in cage, the cakes in frails.

Here, with his children at his side,
  We see the man who, lowly born,
    Rose up from peasant-state to peer,
Who won a princess for his bride,
  Ruled the far leagues of royal corn,
    A prophet-priest of Abusir.

She, who to him was 'beauteous calm,'
  With Thi and Thamut, best of boys,
    Sits by to hear the harpers play,
And 'mistress of his house,' 'the palm
  Of pleasantness,' she still enjoys
    The music of that olden day.

Our lamps are lit, the double room
    Is filled with sound of men and flocks,
        Lowing of kine and bleat of goat.
The asses trample thro' the gloom,
    The butcher ties or slays the ox,
        The busy builder shapes the boat.

The Magistrate with face severe,
    The Bailiff squat with reed and scroll,
        These ply the rod or wield the pen.
Serfs stand before the overseer,
    The labourer comes a living toll,
        God's people were but chattels then.

The reaper cuts the ears of wheat,
    Away their load the asses carry,
        A pannier slips, it all but falls !
There on the threshing floor, the feet
    Of oxen tread the corn, nor tarry,
        ' Trot on, trot on ! ' the driver calls.

Strong pulling for the hornèd teams,
    Strong speed for beast or man or boy,
        Strong labour, strenuous laugh and fun.
Such is the old-world tale that gleams
    From storied wall, pain mixed with joy
        And gladness in their god the Sun.

Yea joy in labour for their lord,—
　　Just friend and generous-hearted master,
　　　　They know his shadow-self has need,
They press the cattle through the ford,
　　They plough and sow and reap the faster,
　　　　To think Thi's soul shall surely feed.　　.

Yet in those days of toil and care
　　Men felt a fever still within
　　　　For something more than daily food.
They flung the boomerang in air,
　　They cast their nets for fowl or fin,
　　　　And fought the monsters of the flood.

Above their heads, with clamour harsh
　　The wild-fowl rise ; and from the nest
　　　　A callow brood sends bitter cry,
For near the tyrant of the marsh,
　　The sacred jackal on his quest,
　　　　Glares at them with his hungry eye.

Lo ! in his light papyrus punt
　　Thi stands gigantic, unafraid,
　　　　To watch his spearmen do their deeds,
Or hook leviathan they hunt,—
　　The mighty plaything God has made,
　　　　The river-horse among the reeds.

With thrust of pole and stab of spears,
    And shout of men the fight goes on—
        Swift mind against brute bulk and slow;
Five thousand and five hundred years
    Have passed, the battle is not won :—
        The man above, the beast below.

Lord of the secret Death unrolls
    Rest in Amenti.   Still is strife,—
        Our earth not yet to peace hath come;
We have not realised our souls,
    As you who for your spirit life
        Made pleasant this ' eternal home.'

Yet Thi, you teach us how men miss
    Their mortal being's plain intent
        Who dream at death new sense is given.
You with your prayer to Anubis
    Felt sure as to the tomb you went
        Earth's heart of joy was joy in Heaven.

XXVII

AT JOSEPH'S TOMB

(SAKKARAH)

BEYOND the ruinous heap of stone and sand
    That one time hid King Teta in its cave,
    Across the beans and lentils looks a grave,
Whose doors wide open stand.

And here, men say, still lingers on the name
    Of him who strongly ruled a stubborn race,
    So gentle-hearted, that he hjd his face
When his young brother came.

And they who gaze from Joseph's tomb, may know
    In truth the dreams that troubled Pharaoh's bed,
    May see the lean kine and the kine full-fed
Pass from the pool below.

But in my dream I hear, far off, the groans
    Of people mad for toil and tyranny,
    Who come with haste and with a bitter cry
To claim their father's bones.

Up from the boats, and thro' the burning sand,
   They seek, deep sunk in earth, the painted chest,
   To bear the heart, that here would never rest,
Home to his native land.

They leave the tomb, they flee the white-walled town,[1]—
   Fearful they came, in trembling haste they go,
   And o'er the land of terror and of woe
Blood-red the sun drops down.

[1] Memphis was spoken of in ancient times as 'the town of the white wall.'

XXVIII

AHMED THE CARPENTER

AHMED, the carpenter, breaker of tombs,
  What was the gain of the task for you—
You who entered the Pyramid wombs,
  Rifled the dwelling of Nefer-as-u?

Was it the mummy in mask of gold
  When you lifted the black sarcophagus lid?
Or wonder of heart and eyes to behold
  The god who builded the Pyramid?

How you tunnelled away in the dark and the heat,
  Slept to dream of the meed and the moil,
Felt the dust was laid with your sweat,
  Saw your hands run red with your toil,—

This is not written; but there are the scars
  Your hammer made, when you broke your way,
Here is your name in the 'Chamber of stars,'
  Ahmed the carpenter,—Fame was your pay!

NOTE.—The name of 'Ahmed the Carpenter' is written in red
paint or ink within one of the chambers of the Pyramid of Unas,
last king of the fifth dynasty, called 'Neferasu,' which lies south-east
of the Step Pyramid at Sakkarah.
  It is generally believed that 'Ahmed' was the man who, about the
year A.D. 820, broke his way into the great Pyramid at Gîzeh.

XXIX

EVENING

(BY THE NILE)

THE dogs are barking at the sun,
    Dark lines of women homeward pass,
    Each bearing on her head sweet grass,
And at their sides the children run.

The buffalo with nose in air,
    The camel grumbling at his load,
    Unbidden take their evening road,
And leave behind the clover square.

Wrapped in their cloud of dust, the sheep
    And laden asses homeward go,
    Within the village wall they know
Will be security and sleep.

And this with plough upon his back,
    And that with wooden hoe in hand,
    The bare-legged scanty-skirted band
Of labourers seek the village track.

No more the wet Sakîyeh wheel
   Above the cotton gleams and burrs,
   The shadûf-pole no longer stirs—
Forsaken for the evening meal.

And stooping from the heaven above,
   While all the air about us sings
   With music of ten thousand wings,
Hies to her towery home, the dove.

xxx

NIGHT WATCHERS

THE night is dark, the stars are bright,
　　Our crew are sleeping sound below,
But on the bank, in ruddy light,
　　The village watchmen's faces glow.

The old man sits, his wrinkles tell
　　He has few watches more to keep ;
His son, and his son's son as well,
　　Crouch by, to guard the strangers' sleep.

The talk burns up, the fire burns down,
　　New flame the broken corn-stalks raise,
And naked limbs, lean, lank, and brown,
　　Are stretched towards a cheerful blaze.

In that cold land from whence we came,
　　We sat beside our fires erewhile,
But never knew the joy of flame
　　Like these poor children of the Nile.

With skirts tucked up to belted waist,
  They huddle round it, knees to chin,
They seem its warm-breathed power to taste,
  They rub its rosy comfort in.

Old Egypt's oracles are dumb,
  Tho' yonder burns the Sothic star,[1]
The Sun-god Horus, Ra, and Tum,
  By Nilus' bank, unworshipped are.

But this red flower of flame that springs
  Is kindred to the rose of morn,
And to these village watchmen brings
  The blessing that with day is born.

Unconscious votaries the band
  Around their burning altar sit,
And offering make, with careful hand,
  And break the fuel, bit by bit.

Then when the mist is white as snow,
  In abbas wrapt the watchmen rise;
Beyond the Arabian hills, they know,
  The dawn prepares its new surprise.

---

[1] From the rising of this star, Sirius, the Egyptians calculated their Sothic year of 365¼ days.

The cocks are crowing in the plain,
　　The pigeons fly, the village wakes,
The girls go forth to weed the grain,
　　The Shadûf-man his bucket takes.

Then to their toil afield they fare,
　　Our guards,—with ne'er a word of thanks,—
And leave behind their seal of care—
　　Black ashes on the silent banks.

XXXI

NILE BOATS

TALL towers of snow, or sloping from the gale,
    With what majestic progress o'er the flood
Pass the great boats that hoist the single sail,
    As if they felt the king was in their blood !—

As if their white similitude of form
    To Upper Egypt's royal crown forth-told
With what ancestral powers they ruled the storm,
    Stemmed Nile's red tide[1] and fought the winds of old.

Yet never more majestical they move,
    Than when, through dazzling sun and flickering rain,
They flash by mounded village, palmy grove,
    And shake their splendours o'er the Delta plain.

For then the silver crown of ancient kings
    By hands of might invisible is borne—
Alternate light and vast o'ershadowings,
    In noiseless triumph thro' the leagues of corn.

---

1 At or near High Nile, the water assumes a red appearance.
Cf. Sir George Airy's *Notes on the Earlier Hebrew Scriptures*, p. 59.

But filled with mystery of magic power
    Seem the great sails that brightened to the noon,
When very silent at the midnight hour
    They glide and gleam against the silver moon.

Then like the wings of some gigantic bird,
    That shine in heaven or dive into the stream,
While scarce a ripple at the prow is stirred,
    They push like phantoms thro' a world of dream.

XXXII

A SCARAB

WITH toil incessant, up the slope,
  The beetle rolls a ball of clay;
  High o'er the water-flood to lay
His egg of hope.

Now broad black head shall push and strain,
  Now mouth shall carry where head fails,
  Now hind, now forward leg prevails
Its end to gain.

The ball rolls back, and back he goes,
  Undaunted heart, unbroken will,
  To bear life's future up the hill
From flood and foes.

Scarab! no marvel men, who are
  So prone to want of will, should see
  A hint of the Divine in thee,—
God Chepera.

No wonder mortals weak in trust,
   Who lay their dear ones in the ground,
   Should feel when scarab-time comes round
No wonder mortals weak in trust,
Some hope in dust.

And if when work is done in part,
   A voice should say, 'Lo, death ends all!'
   The secret of the scarab-ball
May give us heart.

Behold! the glossy shards divide,
   Away the scarabæus flies,
   And leaves, in faith, to sun and skies
His hope, his pride.

XXXIII

THE SHADÛF-MAN

.ALL through the day the red-brown man
   Stands on his perch, in the red-brown bank;
Waters never more gratefully ran,
   Cucumbers never more greedily drank.

A small world his, for the sky is half hidden,
   A pole and a bucket, a mat that streams,
But a world large enough to know what was bidden,
   And to feel that labour is better than dreams.

And the sun goes up, and the sun goes round,
   And round goes the shade of the hurdle o'erhead,
And never a word, and never a sound
   But the splash of the bucket that brings him his bread.

And all the day thro' he bows and bows,
   You may see his broad back bend where he stands,
You might think him a dervish saying his vows,
   Or praying his prayers, as he lifts his hands.

And he hears the marketers hurrying by,
　　Gurgle of camel and pattering hoof,
But not for a moment will cease the cry,—
　　The wheeze and the groan of the long Shadûf.

But I think he knows that the golden grain
　　Is the gift of the strength of his tireless arm,
That, quite unseen, he is felt in the plain,
　　And, quite unknown, he is blessed by the farm.

Oh! not unmindful the good gods are!
　　For him, when the sun has sunk in the west,
The heaven drops into his bucket a star,
　　And he hies him home, and he takes his rest.

XXXIV

THE MARRIAGE OF THE PALMS

Up the rough palm with monkey-toes
And monkey-hands Shêkh Ali goes,
There, girthed with rope, and slung at ease,
He makes the marriage of the trees;
Forth from his bosom see he takes
The magic spathe, and gently breaks,
Then strips the shining ivory bare,
And shakes his beaded wand in air:
Oh! ne'er in August's sunny hours
Came sweeter scent from lime-tree flowers,
Nor at the hives, when clover blooms,
Was air more charged with sweet perfumes,
Than from those tall palm-heads were borne,
When Ali made their marriage morn.
There is no sound of marriage-bell,
The wedding of the trees to tell,
But even the blind old man can say
From fragrance showered upon his way,

That, by the golden dust from heaven,
New hope of fruit for earth is given.
About the palms the children run
Naked and laughing in the sun,
Already in their hearts they feel
Date-harvest here, and fuller meal.
Down Ali comes, his face all smile,
No happier man beside the Nile,
For now, says he, the trees are wed,
And all the village shall be fed.

XXXV

WATER-CARRIERS

(HOPE)

SHWAY-SHWÁYAH, with her lips all blue,
And chin dark-beaded with tattoo,
Takes the large water-jar in hand
And joins the river-going band.
She dreams the one thing good in life
Is to be chosen for a wife :
To-day she wins her fourteenth year,
And if full charged her head can bear
From the far Nile the large ' bellas,' [1]
Straight unto marriage she may pass.
So jauntily she sets aslope
The jar upon her crown of rope :
A man goes by ; with native grace
She draws her veil across her face,
But I could see her dark eyes gleam
With laughter ;—so toward the stream,

---

[1] The large water-jars used by the women to carry water from
the Nile.

With ankle-bracelets jangling loud,
They hurry on, a barefoot crowd.
Then to the water-flood they haste,
The skirts bunched up about their waist,
Fill the large water-jars, and hand
Their shining amphoræ to land;
Raise to the knee, then with a cry
And helpful hoist from standers by,
Set the huge weight upon their head,
Find balance with a forward tread,
And stately, with one hand behind
To hold the burden to the wind,
High-crowned but solemnly and slow
The water-bearers homewards go,
With young Shway-shwáyah pleased to carry
Her full-sized jar—and fit to marry.

XXXVI

WATER-CARRIERS

(JOY)

LIKE huge dark herons thro' the morning mist,
  Bare-legged the women in the shallows stand;
  Deep in the muddy river, with one hand
They sink the water-jars that swirl and twist,
Then with a clever jerking of the wrist
  They scoop in water and keep out the sand,
  And bear the gleaming ' bellas ' safe to land.

But sweet Habeebeh back again will come
  To wash her arms and face and her full lips;
  She laughs, she is a bride, those finger-tips
So red with henna tell she has a home,
And lord; she cleanses next her jar from loam,
  Leaps up the bank, and shakes about her hips
  The flowing robe of blue, and off she trips.

XXXVII

WATER-CARRIERS

(SORROW)

NOT with the villagers at night and morn,
But very sorrowful the lonely mile,
Hadêyeh goes for water to the Nile.

For wedded long, no man-child has been born
Her lord and master's village home to bless,
And all her life is heavy bitterness.

The dreary way she, silent and downcast,
Will plod in grief, but must perforce return
Head up, to bring the heavy household urn.

And every morn she wishes were the last,
But still toward the Nile perforce she goes,
And weeps, and none have pity on her woes.

For all the talk at morn and eventide,
When from the river Nile they water bear,
Is of the plants Egyptian mothers rear.

Of how the camel went for Hasan's bride,—
How the Shêkh's dame was lately brought to bed,
 nd of her firstborn now is lying dead.

To listen to the birds was her delight,
Her eyes were like the hawk's that hangeth over,
She filled her hands with blossom of red clover.

Her ears are duller and her eyes less bright,
With her no more the flowers of spring prevail,
She hardly hears the piping of the quail.

And I have watched the melancholy wife
Stand sobbing, as she heaved the jar ashore,
And prayed she might not see the sunset more.

Have heard her groan, and seen the bitter strife
Wherewith unhelped she lifted up the jar,
And went by starlight home without a star.

XXXVIII

A BUFFALO RIDE

THE hour to leave the field has come,
　　Hamâdi all day in the sun
　　Beside his lop-eared goat has run;
　　Weary of work, and tired of fun,
Now, who shall bear Hamâdi home?

The little lad is fain to ride,
　　Looks longingly toward his mother,
　　But Hamad has a baby-brother,
　　Frail thing, she cannot bear another
Upon her shoulders set astride.

Before them, with a plough-beam, goes
　　The ox who toils to bring them bread;
　　She cries, the creature stops stone dead,
　　And to the dust bends down his head,
Most docile of all buffaloes.

See! to the horns Hamâdi clings,
　　He knows his friend is true and staunch,
　　The great head lifts, and on his paunch
　　The boy creeps up o'er neck to haunch,
And wins with pride a seat for kings.

XXXIX

THE AFTER-GLOW

As sometimes to a dead unwrinkled face
   There comes a flush, by which we partly know
   The beauty of the youth lost long ago—
The glory of life's morning and its grace—
So to this calm unwrinkled heavenly place,
   Where-from the sun sank suddenly below,
   There came a magical mysterious glow,
When death had paled the whole land for a space.

And swift the death-white argent of the west
   Was changed to saffron, saffron burned to gold,
     Gold leapt to rose, rose lightened into flame;
   You might have thought day young that late was old,
Death life, and for his bride in splendour drest
     The undying sun once more a bridegroom came.

XL

PADDY-BIRDS

In the spring, with a lovelier skin
   Leaps and shines the gazelle ;
That the spring gives grace to the blood
   Even a camel can tell.

The swallow is redder of chin,
   More golden the hoopoe's crest,
The kingfisher, poised on the flood,
   Darts with a brighter breast.

But for you, white friends of the plough,
   Beloved of the child with the goat,
Unhurt by the hinds of the farm,
   And blest by the men of the boat.

For you, with your breasts of snow,
   No change in the spring is seen,
White when the harvest is warm,
   White when the corn is green.

Are ye spirits of good and of just,
   Redeemed in the Hall of Truth,
Sent back to a sad, old earth,
   With the joy of an innocent youth?

Bright souls, unsullied by lust,
   As angels, back have ye come
To the darkened land of your birth,
   With the light of a purer home?

XLI

A NILE BOAT-LOAD

Down through the morning mist they go,
We hear the boat-bird's merry crow,
The turkeys chuckle as they pass,
And o'er the bulwark peers the ass,
While the tall camel in the stern
Looks with a large-eyed grave concern;
The mother, catching up her veil,
Peeps at us from behind the sail,
The girl holds up her coral beads,
Up spring the youngsters' tufted heads;
Against the tiller leans the slave,
Shows his white teeth, his hand doth wave,
And old Shêkh Moosa, fresh from sleep,
Upon his date-fruit's purple heap,
Roused by our Reis's cheery cry,
Gives us ' God's Peace,' and so goes by.
But one there is who nothing cares,
Hammad, who, mindful of his prayers,

Squat on the boat's extremest edge,
Beside the giant rudder's ledge,
Pours o'er his shoulder's coppery gleam
The silver tribute of the stream,
Ere he asks God to keep away
Satan, 'accursed with stones' to-day,
And leaves another morning's fate
To Allah, merciful and great.

XLII

A MONKISH SWIMMER

(GEBEL ET-TÊR)

HIGH on their cliff-edge convent-perch[1]
　　They watch—those human birds of prey
For God and Holy Mother Church—
　　They scan the distance far away,
Report what dahabiyehs gleam,
Where move the faint far clouds of steam.

'Ho! Theodorus, strong of limb!
　　To those God-given boats we toil
Thy name is kindred; thou must swim,
　　And from the passengers claim dole.'
So cries the Elder,—Theodore
Goes grumbling down towards the shore.

---

[1] The Coptic convent 'of the Pulley,' Dêr-el-Bakarah, said to
have been founded by the Empress Helena. The patriarch has
forbidden the practice, but alms are still solicited, from time to time,
by sturdy monkish swimmers.

Then when our vessel comes in sight,
   The Coptic Monk he strips him bare,
Guesses the rolling torrent's might
   To aid his course, and breathes a prayer
For safety from the crocodile,
So plunges headlong in the Nile.

Hand over hand with frequent splash
   The swarthy swimmer comes apace,
Now close beneath, his dark eyes flash,
   We see the working of his face;
Another stroke—the rope!—the rope!
He leaps aboard beyond our hope.

In utter nakedness he stands,
   He begs for alms and craves for food,
And shows his cross-imprinted hands,
   Sure token of his brotherhood;
Puts in his mouth what each one gives,
Then sudden from the deck he dives.

Swift come, swift gone, we watch his head
   Slant-wise across the river steer,
We feel his hard-won bit of bread
   A whole community may cheer:
Cast on the waters, lo, how soon
We find our gift regiven boon!

XLIII

AT THE TOMB OF AMENI AMENEMHÂT

(BENI HASÂN)

HERE, conscious of his work well done,
There rests the lady Hennu's son ;
   Who, in his agèd father's place,
   Warred with the Ethiopian race,
Set them their bounds, and to his king,
Usertsen, brought back offering ;
   Chief president of prophets he,
   And nomarch of Antinöe ;
One of old Egypt's feudal lords ;
Now hearken Amenemhât's words.

' Ne'er from my word have I gone,
All that I said I have done.
A gracious, compassionate man,
A governor loving his town.
In Meh all the years of my span
Was I ruler ; I laboured to plan
The palace, the work was mine own.

To the priests of the temple of Meh
Three thousand bulls have I driven,
Three thousand bulls with their cows,
That unto the gods might be given
Gifts and due paying of vows.
Honour had I from the king,
For this that I carried him all
The fruits of the milking stall,
And unto the palace did bring
Milk, white cheeses and whey;
Yea, none contributed more
Than I to the royal store.

Never a child did I harm,
Nor took from a widow her gains,
Nor drove a hind from my gate,
Nor put a herdsman in chains,
Nor impressed from a five-handed farm
Its ploughmen to till for the State.

None were sad in my day,
None went hungry of mouth,
Wretched, or poor at my hand;
If famine threatened to come,
I ploughed all the arable land,
I sowed all the fallows of Meh,
From the northern gate of the Nome
To the frontier lines of the South.

So to the people I gave
Food and provision for life,
None went hungry or bare;
With the widow as with the wife
My doles did I equally share,
The master alike with the slave
Were both of them one in my care;
And if ever the flood was great,
And men grew rich by the yield,
No new taxes or rate
Were laid on the farm and the field.'

NOTE.—One of the most interesting of the northern group of
Rock Tombs at Beni Hasân, which were all hewn at the time of
Usertsen I. of the twelfth dynasty, B.C. 2433 to B.C. 2400, is the
tomb of the son of the lady Hennu, Ameni Amenemhât, one of the
feudal lords of Egypt, chief of the nome of Meh or Antinöe, and
chief president of the prophets. In his youth he was sent to
Ethiopia in the place of his father, who was too old for the task; he
conducted successfully the warlike expedition, settled the frontiers
of the country, and returned with much tribute and spoil. The
pictures on the walls of the tomb, that are fading very fast, owing
to the merciless treatment they have received at the hands of
visitors, represent scenes on the battlefield, which may perhaps
commemorate this expedition; but the pictures of Ameni's life on
the farm, on the river, and in the hunting-ground, interesting as
they are, with their details of Egyptian life when Usertsen was
king, and specially of the part which women played at that time in
domestic pursuits, pass into insignificance before the story of the
man's life and character as given us by himself. This inscription
on his tomb I have rendered into verse from the admirable trans-
lation given us by Mr. Wallis Budge, in his book *The Nile*, p. 168.

XLIV

THE DREAM-CITY OF KHUENÂTEN

(AT TEL EL-AMARNA)

WHO through this solemn wilderness may stray
   Beyond the river and its belt of palm,
   May feel still fresh the wonder and the calm
Of greatness passed away.   .

All the new world of Art with Nature one,
   All the young city's restless upward strife,
   Its higher truth, its happier, homelier life, —
All like a phantom gone.

No more the draughtsman from the furthest Ind
   Casts on the palace-floor his vermeil dyes,
   No more the scribe from clay syllabaries
Will spell Assyria's mind.

Not here the potter from the Grecian Isles
   Throws the new shape or plies the painter's reed,
   No kiln-man melts the glaze or bakes the tiles
Or spins the glassy bead.

The Master-sculptor Bek, from Aptu brought,
  No longer bids his pupil, line on line,
  With copying chisel grave the marble fine
To beauty and to thought.

But he who enters yonder mountain cave
  May see the form of that courageous king,
  Who felt that light was life for everything,
And should outlast the grave.

And that dream-city Khuenâten made—
  The boy-reformer by the banks of Nile
  Who broke with Thebes, her priestly power and guile—
Shall never surely fade.

Still in our desert it renews its youth,
  Still lifts its beauty out of barren sands,—
  City, thought-built, eternal, not with hands,
For Light that lives in Truth.

NOTE.—The recent discoveries by Flinders Petrie at Tel El-
Amarna show that there must have arisen there, about 1400 B.C.,
at the bidding of the young reformer-king, Chut-en-âten, or
Khuenâten ('the glory of the sun'), a city filled with men of new
art, new social and new religious ideas.

The remains of the painted pavements of the palace, with their
glowing colours, their unconventional treatment of natural forms,
the remains of the glass-blowers' shops, the sculpture schools, the

Greek vase fragments, bits of portrait sculpture, as fine in execution as sculpture of the best Greek time, all bespeak that in honour of the new religion of the Sun's-Disk-worshipping king and queen, there must have been gathered here the best art of the time from all parts of the world.

The Tel El-Amarna tablets and bi-lingual syllabaries found show that scribes were engaged to decipher the communications that passed between the courts of Khuenâten and the courts of Assyria. The architect who designed the Temple buildings was Bek, son of Men, who had worked under Amenophis III. at Thebes, or Aptu, as it was called.   Cf. Budge's *Nile*, p. 172.

Young Amen-Hotep IV. broke with the Theban priests and their worship of Amen-Ra to establish a new Thebes in this plain, and to honour the sun's disk as a spirit— the embodiment of the principle of life.   He was not then more than eighteen years old, and died at the age of thirty.   Within a generation after his death his whole city was swept away, but the young reformer's motto still survives, and is found constantly repeated.   It is this, ' Living in Truth.'

XLV

GOING TO ASSIOUT

(A NILE BOATMAN'S SONG)

I WOULD I were at Assiout,
I'd buy myself another suit,
    This worn-out cap, I'd doff it.
The winds of God are blowing cold,
My 'abba' is exceeding old;
    O Allah! O my prophet!

XLVI

BIRD-SCARING

(IN THE PLAIN OF ABYDOS)

LIKE a black ghoul upon his heap
  Of clods, the slinger sits all day ;
That so the harvestman may reap,
  He needs must scare the birds away.

Then up he rises, flings aside
  His ' abba ' of dark camel's hair,
And stands aloft, in strength and pride,
  And shines, bronze-hued of skin, and bare.

He takes his palm-rope sling in hands,
  Puts on his thumb the twisted thong,
Then whirrs, and thro' the humming strands
  The air is shaken into song.

And suddenly a ringing crack
  Above the silent corn is heard,
Forth flies the stone upon its track,
  Forth hies the startled robber-bird.

Ah! would to heaven, above our patch
  Of fruit, for mortals in our day,
Such slinger stood, so true to watch,
  So sure to scare ill thoughts away.

XLVII

A WAYSIDE BABE

(AT BELLIANEH)

MOTHER las gone to a well in the South,
   To look for the camel they lost in the strife;
Who will give to her baby's mouth
   A sweet warm draught of the River of Life?

Here it lies on a heap of clover,
   The sycamore shades it from sun that burns,
A dog from the village watches over,
   Who will feed it till Mother returns?

By there came with a full dark breast
   A woman who lost her babe this morn,
Caught up the child and tenderly pressed
   Its lips to the fountain,—less forlorn,

Passed with tears to her work afield;
   After her came a happier mother,
Gave to the babe a bounteous yield,
   And left it there to cry for another.

Haggard and grey a crone limped by,
  Bearing the ' lebben ' [1] for those who reap ;
Dear babe l she said, my breasts they are dry,
  But my arms can lull you back to your sleep.

So there alone lay the dot of a child,
  Alone with the dog in the wide, wide plain,
Woke, and crowed at the sun, and smiled,
  For he knew that his mother would come again.

And the sun sank down, and the purple mist
  Swam up from the Nile, but the dog watched over ;
And the mother leapt down from her camel, and kissed
  Her boy, and went home with her babe and her clover.

[1] Sour milk.

XLVIII

AT ABYDOS

When the dark barges passed toward the mound,
   Whereunder lay Osiris' sacred head,
   Clapping of hands and chanting for the dead
Ceased, and the pipers' tune, the harpers' sound
Were hushed—there at Abydos none may play,
No sistrum scares dark Typhon far away.

For in the sevenfold-sanctuaried hall,
   Where Seti stands to offer blind-eyed Truth,
   Must all men hear how Ramses in his youth,
Taught by his Father, from the gallery wall
To listening centuries with boy-pride proclaims
Those six-and-seventy great ancestral names.

NOTE.—At Abydos, which was approached by a canal, now
disused, hard by the great burial-mound of Kom-es-Sultân, where it
was said the head of Osiris was buried, may still be seen the beautiful
bas-relief of Seti I. offering an image of the blind Truth or 'Ma'
with the ostrich plume to Osiris; and in the corridor beyond the

seven chapels may be seen Rameses ii., his son, as a lad, wearing the side lock, reciting the names of his seventy-six most illustrious ancestors—the names of whom are engraved in their cartouches upon the wall. This list of names is known as 'the tablet of Abydos,' and was discovered by Dümichen in 1864, during M. Mariette's excavation. It commences with Mena and ends with Seti i. Seti is seen offering incense and fire to the names, and is evidently the instructor of his son, who stands behind him.

At the commencement of all ceremonials in the temple of Abydos music seems to have been forbidden.

XLIX

AT KENEH

THROUGH Keneh's narrow streets we went,
  We heard the humming of the wheel,
Where o'er his work the potter bent.

The kneaded mass he downward threw,
  Dead clay life's instinct seemed to feel,
And into forms of beauty grew.

Thence to the Potter's hill we came,
  That burns like Tophet evermore,
And smells of smoke and smothered flame.

This lined his kiln with shapes of clay,
  That from the pit drew forth his store,
And hurried with his jars away.

The potter's ass, with steady feet,
  And bulged with burdens either side,
Went jostling down the busy street.

The crowd gave way with willing grace,
  Tho' none before his coming cried—
'For the jar-carrier make place !'

The Sun hath put their hearts to school,
  They know the universal need
Of 'kulleh' porous, 'bellas' cool.[1]

We are but as these pots, say they,
  From Allah's hand we all proceed,
To back return as broken clay.

Yea, and tho' made by Allah's hand,
  We from a fiery furnace go
To help or hurt a weary land.

How soon we too are cracked and burst
  With flames that work our being woe,
How much to be more full we thirst !

So with his burden through the town,
  Toward the raft upon the Nile,
The ass unchallenged hies him down.

There from his nets he gives his store
  To clamorous boatmen, rests awhile,
And hies him back in quest for more.

---

1 The 'kulleh' is the small water-bottle used for drinking from ;
the 'bellas' is the large water-jar for household use. The staple
manufacture of Keneh is this pottery.

AT DENDERAH

' Goddess of Denderah, to thee I give
Truth, by the life of Truth we mortals live,
Therefore to thee, a suppliant at thy shrine,
I offer Truth, thy work, for Truth is thine.'

Therewith the King held trembling in the gloom
The kneeling image with the ostrich plume,
And from the dark and incense-breathing nook
The glorious sistrum of the goddess took.

Then Hathor spoke, and Typhon, at the sound,
Fled as it thrilled the sanctuary round ;
While all pure spirits seemed with joy to float
And fill the chamber of the Golden Boat.

With groan and cry and wailing of despair,
Lies shrieked and vanished up the temple stair ;
And I might see the pale and guilty king
Bowed and in tears, a conscience-smitten thing.

The sistrum throbbed, its music seemed to wake
Soul-piercing echoes while the goddess spake,
' Learn, suppliant, learn, in sorrow and in ruth,
True life is bent on Goodness, Beauty, Truth.'

NOTE.—Behind the Chamber of the Golden Boat at Denderah is
a little chapel, central of the five that fill up the temple's extremity,
in the which is the niche that was the Holy of Holies. ' Here,' says
Mariette Bey, 'the King alone could penetrate; here, hidden from
all eyes, was the mysterious emblem of the temple, a large sistrum
of gold.'

The temple, dedicated to Hathor, and built in late Ptolemaic and
Roman times, was, as is clear from the wall-sculptures, dedicated to
her as the embodiment of the Platonic doctrine of the Good, the
Beautiful, the True.

The sistrum was supposed, by its sound, to be able to banish Typhon
and all malignant powers of the air; and to set forth by symbol
that men should always be up and doing, and actively bent on the
business of life.

On entering the sanctuary of the temple, the King is represented
as holding forward the present to the goddess,—a little statue of a
female, kneeling in a vase or basket, her head crowned with an
ostrich plume. This is the image of Truth called ' Ma.' As he
presents it he utters these words :—

' I offer to thee Truth, O Goddess of Denderah, for Truth is
thine own work, for thou art Truth itself.'

LI

A PORTRAIT OF CLEOPATRA.

(DENDERAH)

WHEN Cleopatra's proud victorious face
  Smiled from the stone on Hathor's temple wall,
Did not the sculptor's hand, with trembling, trace
  The form that held her Anthony in thrall?

Not as Augustus Caesar, unconcerned
  Of soul, with passion passionlessly cold,
His heart within his hand must needs have burned
  Who wrought the beauty that our eyes behold.

The vulture head-dress, horns, and plaits of hair,
  The stately neck that pearls of price adorn,
These had he graved for goddesses as fair,
  Yet never carved such lips of love and scorn.

LII

A PAPYRUS HUNT

WITH keen but uncommunicative eyes
   Muhammad sits cross-legged upon the floor;
   Forth from his breast he brings the scarab store,
Asks many questions, gives but few replies.
Then, since he finds me true, he deigns arise,
   With paper lantern swinging, goes before,
   Plies the huge key, and softly opens door,
And leads me through his home's intricacies.

Then listening long if there be any sound,
   While the dark Nubian keeps good watch below,
   His eyes like coals of fire begin to glow,
His fingers loose what carefully was bound
Swathed in fine linen, coarsely wrapped around
   With some old goat-hair cloak to shun all show,
   And thence with reverence, tenderly and slow,
He dares unwind what hands in secret wound.

And while Muhammad whistles with drawn breath,
 The black Osiride figure, a good son,
 Gave for the resting of a priest of On,
Gleams grim and black; then a swift hand beneath
Passes, and from its casket's hollow sheath
 There comes a brown papyrus packet, none
 Have opened since the scribe wrote clear thereon,
With charcoal paint, the date of Ani's death.

Then does Muhammad tremble; he can hear
 Far steps; returning, answers ' all is well! '
 For who such ' Chapters of the Dead ' will sell
The chain, the lash, and prison walls must fear.
' A hundred pounds? say, lord, it is not dear?
 Fifty?   Nay, ten!—nay, the endorsement spell!
 This treasure of great Ramses' day can tell!—
Take it, but swear me blameless'—and I swear.

LIII

AT THE RAMESSEUM

(PICTURES, AND THE POEM OF PENTAUR)

WHERE once the red colossal Pharaoh stood,
   Lord of wide lands and every wondering sail,
   The temple-gates are sculptured with the tale
Of Ramses' valour by Orontes' flood.

Here tents are pitched; the altar stone they raise;
   ' Pra-Hormachu,' the legion of the king
   Sets the shield fence; and in the serried ring
Stalks the tame lion, and the asses graze.

There, all alone, Mi-ammon [1] in his might,
   His heart made strong by ' Monthu,' god of war, [2]
   Scatters the foe like chaff beneath his car,
And puts the Hittite thousands to their flight.

The river runs blood-red by Kadesh towers,
   Like crocodiles they tumble to the stream,
   This is no man that drives them, he doth seem
A god himself with Baal-suteck's powers.

---

[1] One of Ramses' titles of honour, = ' Favourite of Ammon.'
[2] One of the forms of the Sun-god Ra, as warrior-god of Light.

Half drowned they snatch the King of Khilibu
   Forth from the flood, and bring him safe to bank;
   Many drank deep of death that day, none drank
Deeper of Kadesh stream, Old Chief, than you.

Lo, fresh from fight, the Pharaoh on his throne !
   Pricked to the heart, the sycophants must hear
   Royal rebuke and reprimand severe :—
' Ye cravens, wherefore left ye me alone.

Not one among you had the soul of might !
   Cowards, who so forsook me to your shame !
   No prince or captain to my succour came !
Alone I turned the thousands to their flight.'

The gates may fall, the pictures all may fade,
   The battle cannot pass; a poet's tongue
   Is dowered with immortality : one sung
That deed of arms.   Hear now the song he made :—

Then the king of Khita-land,
With his warriors made a stand,
But he durst not risk his hand
In battle with our Pharaoh; so his chariots drew
   away,
Unnumbered as the sand ;
And they stood, three men of war
On each car ;

And gathered all in force
Was the flower of his army for the fight in full array,
But advance he did not dare
Foot or horse.

So in ambush there they lay,
North-west of Kadesh town ;
And while these were in their lair,
Others went forth south of Kadesh, on our midst, their
      charge was thrown
With such weight, our men went down,
For they took us unaware,
And the legion of Pra-Hormakhu gave way.

But at the western side
Of Arunatha's tide,
Near the city's northern wall, our Pharaoh had his place.
And they came unto the king,
And they told him our disgrace ;
Then Rameses uprose, like his father, Month, in might,
All his weapons took in hand,
And his armour did he don,
Just like Baal, fit for fight ;
And the noble pair of horses that carried Pharaoh on,
Lo ! ' Victory of Thebes ' was their name,
And from out the royal stables of great Miamun they
      came.

Then the king he lashed each horse,
And they quickened up their course,
And he dashed into the middle of the hostile Hittite host,
All alone, none other with him, for he counted not
     the cost.
Then he looked behind, and found
That the foe were all around,
Two thousand and five hundred of their chariots of war;
And the flower of the Hittites, and their helpers, in a ring—
Men of Masu, Keshkesh, Pidasa, Malunna, Arathu,
Qazauadana, Kadesh, Akerith, Leka and Khilibu—
Cut off the way behind,
Retreat he could not find;
There were three men on each car,
And they gathered all together, and closed upon the king.
'Yea, and not one of my princes, of my chief men and
     my great,
Was with me, not a captain, not a knight;
For my warriors and chariots had left me to my fate,
Not one was there to take his part in fight.'

Then spake Pharaoh, and he cried: 'Father Ammon,
     where art thou?
Shall a sire forget his son?
Is there aught without thy knowledge I have done;
From the judgments of thy mouth when have I gone?

Have I e'er transgressed thy word?

Disobeyed, or broke a vow?

Is it right, who rules in Egypt, Egypt's lord,

Should e'er before the foreign peoples bow,

Or own their rod?

Whate'er may be the mind of this Hittite herdsman-horde,

Sure Ammon should stand higher than the wretch who
    knows no God?

Father Ammon! is it nought

That to thee I dedicated noble monuments, and filled

Thy temples with the prisoners of war?

That for thee a thousand years shall stand the shrines
    I dared to build?

That to thee my palace-substance I have brought?

That tribute unto thee from afar

A whole land comes to pay?

That to thee ten thousand oxen for sacrifice I fell,

And burn upon thine altars the sweetest woods that smell?

That all thy heart required my hand did ne'er gainsay?

I have built for thee tall gates and wondrous works,
    beside the Nile,

I have raised thee mast on mast,

For eternity to last,

From Elephantin's isle

The obelisks for thee I have conveyed;

It is I who brought alone

The everlasting stone;

It is I who sent for thee,
The ships upon the sea,
To pour into thy coffers the wealth of foreign trade;
Is it told that such a thing
By any other king,
At any other time, was done at all?
Let the wretch be put to shame
Who refuses thy commands,
But honour to his name
Who to Ammon lifts his hands.
To the full of my endeavour,
With a willing heart for ever,
I have acted thus for thee,
And to thee, great God, I call;
For behold! now, Ammon, I,
In the midst of many peoples all unknown,
Unnumbered as the sand,
Here I stand,
All alone;
There is no one at my side,
My warriors and chariots afeared
Have deserted me; none heard
My voice, when to the cravens I, their king, for succour
    cried.
But I find that Ammon's grace
Is better far to me
Than a million fighting men and ten thousand chariots be.

Yea, better than ten thousand, be they brother, be they
    son,
When with hearts that beat like one,
Together for to help me they are gathered in one place.
The might of men is nothing, it is Ammon who is lord,
What has happened here to me is according to thy word,
And I will not now transgress thy command;
But alone, as here I stand,
To thee my cry I send,
Unto earth's extremest end,
Saying, 'Help me, father Ammon, against the Hittite
    horde.'

Then my voice it found an echo in Hermonthis' temple-
    hall,[1]
Ammon heard it, and he came unto my call;
And for joy I gave a shout,
From behind, his voice cried out,
'I have hastened to thee, Ramses Miamun,
Behold! I stand with thee,
Behold! 'tis I am he,
Own father thine, the great god Ra, the sun.
Lo! mine hand with thine shall fight,
And mine arm is strong above

---

[1] At Hermonthis, called the 'An of the South'—modern Erment
—stood a great temple to Monthu, the warrior-god of Light, the
ancient tutelar Lord of Thebes.

The hundreds of ten thousands, who against thee do unite,
Of victory am I lord, and the brave heart do I love,
I have found in thee a spirit that is right,
And my soul it doth rejoice in thy valour and thy might.

Then all this came to pass, I was changèd in my heart
Like Monthu, god of war, was I made,
With my left hand hurled the dart,
With my right I swung the blade,
Fierce as Baal in his time, before their sight.
Two thousand and five hundred pairs of horses were
  around,
And I flew into the middle of their ring,
By my horse-hoofs they were dashed all in pieces to
  the ground,
None raised his hand in fight,
For the courage in their breasts had sunken quite,
And their limbs were loosed for fear,
And they could not hurl the dart,
And they had not any heart
To use the spear;
And I cast them to the water,
Just as crocodiles fall in from the bank,
So they sank.
And they tumbled on their faces, one by one;
At my pleasure I made slaughter,
So that none

E'er had time to look behind, or backward fled;
Where he fell did each one lay
On that day,
From the dust none ever lifted up his head.

Then the wretched king of Khita, he stood still,
With his warriors and his chariots all about him in a ring,
Just to gaze upon the valour of our king
In the fray.
And the king was all alone,
Of his men and chariots none,
To help him, but the Hittite of his gazing soon had fill,
For he turned his face in flight, and sped away.
Then his princes forth he sent
To battle with our lord,
Well equipped with bow and sword
And all goodly armament,
Chiefs of Leka, Masa, Kings of Malunna, Arathu,
Qar-qâ-mash, of the Dardani, of Keshkesh, Khilibu.
And the brothers of the king were all gathered in one
     place,
Two thousand and five hundred pairs of horse—
And they came right on in force,
The fury of their faces to the flaming of my face.

Then, like Monthu in his might,
I rushed on them apace,

And I let them taste my hand
In a twinkling moment's space.
Then cried one unto his mate,
' This is no man, this is he,
This is Suteck, god of hate,
With Baal in his blood ;
Let us hasten, let us flee,
Let us save our souls from death,
Let us take to heel and try our lungs and breath.'
And before the king's attack
Hands fell, and limbs were slack,
They could neither aim the bow, nor thrust the spear,
But just looked at him who came
Charging on them, like a flame.
And the king was as a griffin in the rear
(Behold thus speaks the Pharaoh, let all know), .
' I struck them down, and there escaped me none.
Then I lifted up my voice, and I spake,
Ho! my warriors, charioteers,
Away with craven fears,
Halt, stand, and courage take,
Behold I am alone,
Yet Ammon is my helper and his hand is with me now.

When my Menna, charioteer, beheld in his dismay
How the horses swarmed around us, lo! his courage
    fled away,

And terror and affright

Took possession of him quite;

And straightway he cried out to me, and said,

'Gracious lord and bravest king, saviour-guard

Of Egypt in the battle, be our ward;

Behold we stand alone, in the hostile Hittite ring,

Save for us the breath of life,

Give deliverance from the strife,

Oh protect us, Ramses Miamun! Oh save us, mighty
    king!'

Then the king spake to his squire, 'Halt! take courage,
    charioteer,

As a sparrow-hawk swoops down upon his prey,

So I swoop upon the foe, and I will slay,

I will hew them into pieces, I will dash them into dust;

Have no fear,

Cast such evil thought away!

These godless men are wretches that in Ammon put
    no trust!'

Then the king, he hurried forward, on the Hittite host
    he flew,

'For the sixth time that I charged them,' says the king
    —and listen well,

'Like Baal in his strength, on their rearward, lo! I fell,

And I killed them, none escaped me, and I slew, and
    slew, and slew.'

NOTE.—This, the most remarkable of old Egyptian epics, was written by a court poet of the nineteenth dynasty, Pentaur, in the seventh year of Rameses II., B.C. 1326, and describes the single-handed combat of the great Pharaoh against the Hittites. Its text is preserved on the walls of Abydos, Karnak, Luxor, the Ramesseum and Ipsambul. But it is to the Ramesseum we turn for illustrations of the poem.

Mariette Bey tells us: 'The scene is laid in Syria, on the banks of a river which everything seems to point out as the Orontes. Rameses is present in person, and comes fully armed, to dispute possession of the country, designated under the generic name of the Khetas. Kadesh is the nearest town. Through a concourse of circumstances, which do not reflect credit on the Egyptian generals, Rameses finds himself surrounded by his enemies. The soldiers who formed the escort have taken flight. Rameses stands alone, and no one is with him.'

With unreflecting valour he throws himself among the chariots. He kills the chiefs of the 'vile Khetas,' forces their troops to recross the river in hot haste, and by personal courage turns the threatened rout into a complete victory. This brilliant feat of arms is what the first pylon of the Ramesseum commemorates.

On one side Rameses is seen precipitating himself into the thickest of the fight. The enemy fly in terror; some are crushed under the feet of the horses and under the chariot-wheels; some lie dead on the ground, pierced with arrows shot by the king's own hand; others again leap into the river and are drowned. On the opposite side the king is represented seated on his throne. His officers come forward tendering their congratulations; but it is with reproofs the king receives them. 'Not one among you,' he exclaims, 'has behaved well in thus deserting me, and leaving me alone in the midst of the enemy. The princes and the captains did not join hands with me in fight. I have put to flight thousands of nations, and I was all alone.'

On the interior façade of the second pylon, one may see, by the evening light, the same king in the thick of the battle. Here Grabatousa, the armour-bearer of the Prince of Khita, falls pierced by the arrows of the king; there Rabsounna, captain of the archers, meets with the same fate. The Orontes lies in the path of the Khita, who fly in disorder. Upon one of the pylons one notices the square camp of the Egyptians, surrounded by its wall of shields, which the Egyptian warriors have placed around it. The life of the camp servants, resting by their baggage, comes before us. The asses, some of them giving a little trouble, are loose within the enclosure. Pharaoh's tent is seen in the midst of the camp. The favourite lion ' Tearer-in-pieces,' stalks about, and near it is the shrine of the great gods of Egypt. When one reads the poem of Pentaur, one realises that all this last picture represents the encampment of the first legion of Ammon, the bodyguard of the king, that gave way so disastrously on the great day of battle.

Another wall-sculpture gives us a spirited picture of the battle at the critical moment of Rameses' single-handed victory. The river Orontes runs round two sides of the picture, and the flight of the Hittites' horses and chariots towards the stream, the falling into it of the pursued, as crocodiles fall into the water, is graphically pourtrayed. A copy of this battle-scene is given in Eber's *Egypt*, vol. ii. p. 279.

The papyrus from which this poem was originally translated is known as the third Sallier papyrus, one of several that were purchased from an Egyptian sailor by M. Sallier of Aix, in Provence. It is now in the British Museum. It is a copy of an earlier document. It was seen by Champollion in 1833, but to Vicomte de Rouget belongs the credit of having first attempted a full translation of it, in the year 1856.

Mr. Goodwin translated it in 1858, and Professor Lushington's translation of it is given in vol. ii. of *Records of the Past*, p. 65.

Henry Brugsch Bey, after comparing the various texts of the poem on the monuments, and papyri fragments, and having carefully studied the well-known papyrus of the British Museum, has produced a very full translation, a portion of which is here metrically rendered.

Readers should compare Brugsch Bey's translation (*History of the Pharaohs*, vol. ii. p. 53) with that of Professor Lushington.

Cf. Rawnsley's ' Notes for the Nile,' among *The Hymns of Ancient Egypt*, p. 207 (W. Heinemann : London).

LIV

IN A KING'S TOMB

(BIBAN EL MÛLUK)

OH, if I had been the soul of a king
   Built up in a painted charnel cave,
My hands would have tried wide open to fling
   The prison gate of my stifling grave.

And down thro' the valley of herbless heat
   I should surely have sought the blossoming plain ;
There sat among clover, and cool green wheat,
   And nevermore back have returned again.

For crocodile jaws and serpents of flame,
   And pigs and purgatorial fires
Are well in their way, but the texts are the same ;
   Of ' Āpepi's ' folds [1] one very soon tires.

---

[1] The serpent 'Āpepi,' or Apophis, as the spirit of evil and destroyer of the light, is seen figured in many tombs, notably in the tomb of Seti I., called Belzoni's.

And the soul escaped from the body's thrall
    Had little need more of lounging chairs,[1]
Of harpers harping upon the wall,
    Of pots of unguent and funeral wares.

And loosed from the flesh that has felt Death's sting,
    And freed from the body's anguish and strife,
One would give all the painter's imagining
    For a vision of growth and of painless life.

[1] Visitors to the tomb of Rameses III.—Bruce's tomb—will remember the chairs, harpers, unguents, etc. referred to.

LV

QUEEN HATASU

SPAIN honoured Isabella, England owned
    No queenlier lord than great Elizabeth ;
But when in Egypt Hatasu was throned,
    The ancient East for wonder held its breath.

For this was she who cast aside the veil
    Of sex, fresh courage for her land to bring ;
Rode forth to view her armies, clad in mail,
    And went, in peace, apparelled like a king.

This was the queen who sent her shipmen wide
    New spoil in unknown forest-wilds to hunt,
Gold, ivory, apes and peacocks in their pride,
    And full-grown 'camphors' from the land of Punt.

The queen who 'neath the burning Theban hill
    Set up her terraced temple's gleaming state,
And bade thereon the sculptor's utmost skill
    Her tale of venturous royalty relate.

But we who stand in Karnak's ruined shrine,
   Where shattered now her rose-red obelisk lies,
May view the glory of her brow divine,
   And almost feel the flashing of her eyes.

Beneath the pyramid-peaks of those twin towers,—
   The stateliest ever from Syene brought,
The graver set the seal of all his powers,
   Her fair strong face for whom a whole world wrought.

NOTE.—Hatasu, or Hatshepset, daughter of Thothmes I., sister of Thothmes II. and Thothmes III., B.C. 1600, was one of the most remarkable of the Egyptian queens.

Brugsch tells us in his *Egypt under the Pharaohs*, vol. i. p. 349, that scarcely had her royal brother and husband closed his eyes, when the proud queen threw aside her woman's veil, and appeared in all the splendour of Pharaoh as a born king. For she laid aside her woman's dress, clothed herself in man's attire, and adorned herself with the insignia of royalty. Visitors to Deir-el-Bahari will have noticed the unconventional style of her terraced Temple, and will remember the sculptured scenes that depict the return of the expedition from the land of Punt; will have noted the apes in the rigging of the vessels, the camphor trees, root and all, in huge baskets, which are being unloaded. The construction of this marvellous temple was intrusted to an architect called Senmut, who was much honoured by the queen. Those who have examined the fragments of the fallen obelisk, which he set up in honour of 'Father Amen' at Karnak, will have noted the proud and beautiful face of the queen engraved beneath the pyramidion.

This obelisk and its sister, still standing, respectively, 93 feet and 105 feet high, were hewn in the Syene quarries and brought down to Thebes in seven months. Their beauty of workmanship was as remarkable as their size.

LVI

HOW THE COLOSSI CAME TO THEBES

It was a day of wonder and amaze,
When, looming large above the silver haze,
Far shadowing all the flood,
Great Amenhotep's huge Colossi came,
To honour everlasting the name,
Of Amenoph, the lion-hunter good,[1]
Him and his queenly dame.

Then to his barge stepped swiftly down the king.
'Bring wreaths,' said he, 'rich garments and a ring,
For I would show him grace,
Great son of Hapoo, he who dared alone
To loose these giants from the red-brown stone,
And float them to their Theban resting-place,
Each seated on his throne.'

The oars flashed forth and bent like osier wands
Within the rowers' eager-hearted hands,

---

[1] Memorial scarabæi tell us that Amenoph III. speared 210 lions with his own hand in his hunting expeditions in the land of Naharain.

Their king he leads the van!
Ten thousand boats behind his vessel throng,
With sound of lute and sistrum, harp and song:
Ne'er had such statues by the hand of man
Been borne in pomp along.

There on the shore were gathered from afar
A motley rout, the noble in his car,
The poor man on his ass;
Down the sphinx-avenue[1] was crush and crowd,
Lifting of hands and shouts of wonder loud,
The veriest beggar, humblest lad and lass,
Felt on that day more proud.

High upon Apé's[2] many-gated wall
Shone the bright flags from masts of cedar tall,
The priests, in pard-skins dressed,
And linen garments gleaming in the sun,
Did to the vast propylon tower-heads run,
And gazed on these new glories for the west,
And cried, ' Well done!—well done! '

E'en they who chipped the stone, and mortar made
For Amenhotep's pillared colonnade
Beside the river flood,[3]

---

[1] The Sphinx ' dromos ' that ran between Karnak and Luxor.

[2] Apé, Apts, Aptu, or Aptet, was the old name of Thebes to east of river, comprising Karnak and Luxor.

[3] Amenoph III. built the Temple at Luxor, B.C. 1500, on foundation walls that rose right out of the river.

Left hod; and of the lash no more afeared,
Ceased for a moment from their work and peered,
And saw the sun on throne, broad back, and hood,
As to the hills they steered.

But those eight rafts whereon the statues rode
Moved slow for all two thousand boatmen towed
And stoutly stretched the strands ;
While in the lap of each, to give the time,
A singer stood, and rising to his rhyme
And falling to the clapping of his hands
The oars made ceaseless chime.

Then round the shore beneath the ' Coffin hill ' [1]
Swarmed a dark crowd, of gazing to have fill ;
The dead men all that day
Were left half-wrapped in cerecloth; no one poured
Resin and oil, or in cold bosoms stored
Unguent and spice, for all must hie away
To see those huge Colossi safely shored.

And when the sun had sunk beyond the height,
And the tall cliffs with amethystine light
Gleamed to the after-glow,
The solemn statues slowly eastward turned,
And like to gods of gold their shoulders burned ;

---

[1] The ancient name of the hill to the west of the necropolis at
Thebes, at whose feet the city of the embalmers lay.

And the two thousand rowers ceased to row,
Their rest well had they earned.

So to their place the mighty Memnons came,
And the king called on Amen-Ra by name
To 'stablish the design
Of Hapoo's son ; whose work would magnify
Thebes till the world end, and who set hard by
The king's feet, Mut-em-ua mother divine,
And his queen-consort Thi.

NOTE.—The statues which represent Amenhotep III. in a sitting position, having at their feet statues of his wife Mut-em-ua and of his mother Thi, stand 22 feet apart. The most northerly—the Vocal Memnon—partially destroyed by earthquake, B.C. 27, was repaired by the Emperor Septimius Severus. They are 62 feet high, were carved each out of single blocks of red-brown sandstone grit, probably in the quarries of Jebel Silsileh, floated down here at high Nile, and placed in front of a great temple, now destroyed, B.C. 1500-1465.

The work was executed by a certain Amenhotep, surnamed Hui, son of Hapoo and the Lady Atoo, whose granite portrait-statue is preserved in the Gîzeh Museum. From the inscription on that statue we know the history of this remarkable man. Speaking of these Colossi, he says : 'I caused to be built eight ships; then the statues were carried up the river, and placed in their sublime building. They will last as long as Heaven.'

'I declare to you, who shall come here after us, that of the people assembled for the building, all were under me. They were full of ardour, their heart was moved with joy, they raised a shout, they praised the gracious God. Their landing in Thebes was a joyful event.'

Cf. Brugsch's *Egypt under the Pharaohs*, vol. i. p. 427.

LVII

AN INSCRIPTION ON THE VOCAL MEMNON

ITALY my native place,
Dillius my father's name,
I, Petronianus, came
With an offering to thee,
Elegiacs—for the grace
Of the god who speaks to me—
Gift of song and singer's fame.

Grant me in return, O king,
Happy length of days to gain!
Many pilgrims come with pain
Seeking Memnon's place, to know
f he still have power to sing,
Wondering if a voice be now
In the limbs that still remain.

As for him upon his throne
Sitting headless, still he sighs,
To his mother still he cries
Shame on fierce Cambyses' hand;
Still of day's return his tone
Tells to all who near him stand,
Soon as sun-shafts pierce the skies.

NOTE.—The inscriptions on the legs of the Colossus mostly date from between the times of Nero and Septimius Severus. Many are in prose, a few are in verse. The translation above given is of one of the latter form.—Cf. Mariette Bey's *Monuments of Upper Egypt*, p. 199. It is of interest in showing that at the time it was written, Cambyses, and not the earthquake, was believed to be the destroyer, and that the Memnon had not yet been repaired.

LVIII

QUAILS AND THE VOCAL MEMNON

(THEBES)

HARK to the sound of it, piping so merrily,
　　Quavering chirrup and note of the bird,
　　　Clear in the clover, all the plain over,
Just the same voice of the Spring that verily
　　Taia the beautiful queen [1] once heard.

Look at the flight of it, frolic and fluttering,
　　Speckle of breast and brown of the wing,
　　　Each to his lover, that calls in the clover,
Just the same tale of his happiness uttering
　　Now, as when Amenoph great was the king.

Sound of it, sight of it, flutter and flight of it!
　　Memnon no more makes his music at morn—
　　　This little lover, ubiquitous rover,
Never has ceased from his song and delight of it,
　　Since in the valley was clover and corn.

---

[1] Visitors to the Gîzeh Museum will remember the beautiful
limestone head of this queen. Her portrait is well preserved in her
tomb at Thebes. Cf. V. Stuart's *Nile Gleanings*, Plates xx. xxi.

LIX

HABEEBEH'S LOVE

(EDFU)

THE mad old Shêkh with hungry eye
    Has claimed Habeebeh for his own ;
'Three cows,' said he, ' the girl may buy,
    And give her sire a broidered gown.'

The shêkh may make her body his—
    Her body lithe and fresh and fair,
Habeebeh has a heart, and this
    The shêkh, he cannot buy nor share.

For Mustapha, who mends the boats,
    Has seen her to the river come,
Has watched her watering the goats,
    And followed to her father's home.

And many a day, beside the Nile,
    Has helped her hoist the water-jar,
Through toil and heat has thought the while
    At sunset shines my evening star !

He was her giant, strong and kind,
   She was to him his village dove,
But neither spake.　He felt her mind,
   And she—she only guessed his love.

But when the sugar-cane was sweet,
   Forth from his breast a piece he drew,
Brake it, and gave her part to eat,
   Kept part, and so his love she knew.

Thereafter, through the springing corn,
   Or with the quails among the clover,
Habeebeh felt new hope was born,
   And happier skies were bending over.

Thereafter, when the bean-fields bloom,
   A sweeter fragrance filled the air,
More welcome was the star-lit gloom,
   The sun shone every morn more fair.

Three cows and an embroidered gown !—
   What father could resist the price ?
A crier ran throughout the town,
   They bruised the henna, boiled the rice.

Forth went the old shêkh's camel, gay
   With cowrie trappings, plume and bell,
Habeebeh could no longer stay,—
   She had no heart to say farewell.

And entering there by Edfu's gate,
   Above her crimson bridal shawl
She saw her lover watch and wait,
   She spake not, but her eyes spake all.

A whole year long she never smiled,
   And then she knew a mother's joy;
But once in dream, she muttered, ' Child,
   Thou art mine own dear lover's boy.'

The old shêkh rose from off his mat,
   He clutched the babe with hideous cry,
He cursed it, in her face he spat,
   And said, ' To-morrow thou shalt die 1

' Was it for this the torches burned,
   For this the zikr [1] filled the street,
For this, thou thrice-divorced and spurned
   From home, we hired the zaghareet? ' [2]

To-morrow came, the town was moved,
   The Kâdi [3] called accusers four,
Habeebeh went, for him she loved
   Condemned, toward the river shore.

---

[1] The frantic dance of the dervishes, often performed at weddings.
[2] Shrill cries of joy made by women hired for the occasion.
[3] The Judge. On such occasions the evidence of four distinct accusers was necessary to procure conviction.

They screamed from roof, they cast the dust,
　　Dogs barked, and women yelled their hate,
But she in Allah put her trust,
　　In Allah, the Compassionate.

And never proudlier stepped a bride
　　To bathe upon her wedding morn,
For Mustapha was at her side,
　　And death were easy to be borne.

They walked in silence, two but one,—
　　What life had joined could dying sever?
She hardly felt the chain and stone
　　To sink her from his sight for ever.

Then while the drawling-voiced Fikee [1]
　　Pronounced the doom to endless hell,
Habeebeh turned one face to see,
　　And heard a murmur, 'All is well.'

Yea, all is well—a wild shout rang,
　　Habeebeh sank before their eyes,
And Mustapha, the lover, sprang
　　To join his love in Paradise.

---

[1] The village schoolmaster and lay reader of the Koran.

LX

AT KOM OMBO

BEYOND the mountain gateway ' of the chain,' [1]
    That held in bonds the surly-flowing river,
Till Pharaoh paid to Hâpi vows again,
    And 'stablished feasts for ever. [2]

There lies a bank of yellow-golden sand,
    Where-from a tower falls crumbling to the tide,
Above, half hid, two sanctuaries stand,
    Twin temples side by side. [3]

In one was Evil honoured, in one Good,
    Hymns to Light there, and here to Dark were raised,
In both that subtle dragon of the flood,
    The crocodile, was praised.

[1] Hagur or Jebel Silsileh.

[2] The Nile—Hâpi—was worshipped here. Rameses II. re-established the Nile festival, and set up a temple at this point to the river-god.

[3] Founded by Ptolemy VII.—Philometor, B.C. 170 to 146, and dedicated to Horus and Sebek.

And looking forth from 'neath the portico,
  Where overhead the wingèd sun-disc flew,
I could not wonder Light was worshipped so,
  It was so fair a view.

But when the gleaming river changed to grey,
  And stars upon the shallows glistened bright,
I felt that unto Darkness I could pray,
  So glorious was the night.

Who knows, within the breast of those who built,
  Was some fore-knowledge that the human heart
Perplexed by possibilities of guilt,
  Must choose the better part.

That powers of darkness, venomous and great,
  With powers of light must be at endless strife,
If Man would grow the master of his fate,
  And win the higher life.

Or had the souls who set this double shrine
  Some vision of that Hebrew prophet's sight,
'The day and night, O Lord! they both are Thine,
  Alike, the dark and light.' [1]

Ps. cxxxix. 12.

LXI

A POTSHERD AT ELEPHANTINE

THE river broadens into calm,
    And runs from roaring into rest,
        Where underneath the purple skies
        Of evening, clear reflected lies
    Upon the water's burnished breast,
A double island, rock and palm.

Beyond—is famine and is fear,
    The sorrow of the waste Soudan,
        The Mahdi's wrath, the sabre's flash;
        Beyond,—the torrent's foam and crash,
    But here is quiet Assuan,—
Food, peace, security is here.

By ancient Abu [1] as I stroll,
    Where once the ivories were stored,
        I hear Syene's quarry ring
        With hammer-strokes for queen and king,
    The sledge is dragged, the water poured,
The red Colossi shoreward roll.

[1] The old name for the island of Assuan was Abu = the Elephant.

In vain I seek the Sun-god's well,
   O'er which, at high meridian, stood
      Râ's golden boat that sought the west;
      Osiris has been dispossest,
   Tho' from his hand men take their food
They will not here his praises tell—

Nor wonder, seeing how the dust
   Is sown with tax and toll for bread;
      The very sherds beneath our feet
      Cry, 'Ere the men of Kush may eat,
   The lords of Egypt shall be fed!
The Roman Eagle have his lust!'

And wandering on by Pêpi's stone,
   I pluck from out the ruinous heap
      A tile whereon some Grecian wrote;
      What tax-collector struck the note,
   That, echoing, makes our hearts to leap
With music of old Homer's tone?

For all the world of toil and fret,
   Of foes that still with might assail,
      Of tax still forced by tyrant's hand,
      Is charmed to silence as we stand
   To hear the fragmentary tale
Of Troy, no centuries can forget.

NOTE.—The broken potsherds that are strewn in such abundance
in one part of the island of Elephantine, written with ancient Greek,
are now ascertained to be the receipts given by the Government
tax-collector during the Roman occupation of Egypt, A.D. 77-165,
for the merchandise of Nubia as it entered Egypt at Elephantine.

The very name of the island suggests that here may have been
stored in olden days the ivories brought from the lands of Kush
and Punt.

Among the potsherd fragments have been found one or two in-
scribed with portions of Homer's Iliad; one with an extract from
the eighteenth book of the Iliad is preserved in the Louvre. It is to
this fact that an allusion is made in the poem.

The boulder stone inscribed with the names of Pêpi and other
kings of the sixth dynasty will be familiar to travellers, but no
trace remains of the famous 'Well of the sun,' which was said to
be entirely enlightened by the sun's rays at noon from top to bottom,
and which was believed to mark the world's meridian, as the sun
cast no shadow there at noon.

LXII

SHOOTING THE CATARACT

WE heard the mighty river roar,
  But safe in Moussa's dext'rous hand·
Were swirled ashore,
  To find the naked village band
  Jet-black against the ·yellow sand.

Their chieftain bids them stand in rank;
  How ·many will the stranger pay
To leave the bank,
  And let the torrent bear away
  Body and soul, if need be? say !

All at a piastre ahead
  Shall shoot the cataract this noon
Alive or dead !
  The white lord grants a. white lord's boon,
  They shout, and doff their shark-skin shoon.

Then on along the shore they race:
   This, with a log whereon to ride,
Of swiftest pace
   His water-horse he will bestride
   And gallop down the foaming tide;

And that, without a horse of wood,
   Will with the torrent dare to strive,
Into the flood
   With nothing but a flag will dive
   To tell us he is still alive.

And by them run the baby boys,
   With little bellies bladder-tight;
Their father's joys,
   They laugh,—the cataract has no fright
   For babes accustomed to the sight.

Then with a leap and with a yell,
   Like creatures of some riverkind,
Their bodies fell
   Into the whirlpool: I was blind,
   A sudden fear possessed my mind.

But in a moment thro' the spite
   Of furious waters, head by head,
Leapt into light;
   I saw the flags flash into red,
   As down the cataract they sped.

Spurned from the flood or sucked beneath,
   And nerved with more than natural force
They fenced with death;
   Proud riders of the wooden horse
   They went in triumph down the course.

My brain nigh whirled, my ears were stunned,
   But half-mile away, where sand
In stillness sunned
   Its golden breast, the swarthy band
   Swam safe and shining-wet to land.

LXIII

AT PHILAE

(A PROPHECY)

ABOVE the palms uprose a temple fair
   The Grecian monarch for Osiris made,
You well might think that down the water stair
   Would throng the priests, or fill the colonnade,
For Nectanebo—last of all his line—
Had come to view the building of his shrine;

Might dream of Cleopatra,[1] she whose name,
   Graved on her obelisk, became the key
Whereby men read of Egypt, and the fame
   Of those old days, before Arsinoë
Bade Philadelphus unto Isis rear
His splendid ' Hall for Lamentations ' here.

The solemn boatman stretched a jet-black hand,
   Such hand as clasped of old the heavy oar,
And night and day went upward through the sand
   Of Nûb, to row from Philae's holy shore

---

[1] Champollion, by means of this name on the obelisk at Philae, since carried away to Corfe Castle, Dorset, discovered an important key to hieroglyphics.

K

Once in the year, great Isis, borne to bless
The Ethiop in his burning wilderness.[1]

I stepped to land, I passed the towered gate
   Where the fierce Ptolemy lifts his axe of might,
Saw thro' the gloom the chapel walls [2] relate
   Of Horus born to slay the dark by light,
And heard the parable of song made plain,
That tames the hand and bids it sow the grain.

Thence ent'ring to the pillared palms up-grown
   With fronds of glorious colour, fadeless still,
I found our King of Light and Peace had sown
   To sound of song his seed of gracious will,
That here one time the worshipper was fed
By Him who came from Heaven, to be Earth's bread.[3]

---

[1] The Blemyes, an ancient Ethiopic nation, had the privilege of conveying each year, from the sanctuary of Philae, the image of the goddess Isis to visit their temples in the land of Nub. Philae, after the desertion of Abydos, became the centre of Osirian worship. It was called 'The Holy Island.'

[2] Horus is seen listening to music at his mother's knee, and afterwards sowing grain.

[3] Within the painted portico of the large temple may be seen a credence table and aumbry with the cross upon them. The Copts under Abbot Theodore appear to have taken possession of the island at the end of the fifth century. Travellers will remember the Christian basilica north-west of the temple.

Feed us, I cried, with that sweet Food of yore,
    And bid this island sanctuary hear
Again the oath by which old Egypt swore,
    'By Him who sleeps in Philae,'[1] chanted clear;
Let God awake! for Isis, Christ return,
And pour His peace to Nilus' troubled urn!

E'en as I prayed, above the sorrowful sound
    Of nations weary for their warrior hates,
Men sang, 'The Prince of Peace again is crowned;
    Lift up your heads, ye everlasting gates!
Where the Hawk-god of Ethiopia[2] pined,
Where Isis lingered late,[3] is Christ enshrined.'

I gazed across the flood to that dark stone—
    Great 'Pharaoh's seat,'—I heard the river cry,
Methought a mightier King is on his throne,
    A stronger stream henceforward passes by,
The cataract dooms of Death may bellow near,
Lo! Christ has come,—and Life and Peace are here.

[1] The most solemn oath by which an Egyptian could swear was 'By Him who sleeps in Philae,' being an allusion to the reputed burial of the body of Osiris on the island.

[2] Strabo saw the sacred hawk of Ethiopia when he visited Philae. It was then nigh sick unto death.

[3] The worship of Isis lingered at Philae as late as A.D. 453, 74 years after the edict of Theodosius, which abolished the Egyptian religion elsewhere.

LXIV

THE MAHDI'S MESSAGE

MARCH 11, 1884

'Nothing can be between us but the sword;
    The Mahdi's sword above your heads must be,
    And on your necks where'er your hosts shall flee
God's iron!' So fierce Osman's passionate word
Flamed at us; and behind it flashed the horde
    Of men who, strong in Allah's one decree,
    Rose like a wave of darkness from the sea,
Sank like a wave that on the sand is poured.

Dead faces stare up furious from the dust;
    Wild mouths, fixed firm for that last battle-cry,
        Seem shouting, 'Allah! Allah! Allah!' still,
    Fierce men whom Wrong had armed with bravery,
        Whose faith in God no bullet-showers could kill.—
Only the Sword between us?   Let it rust!

Printed by T. and A. Constable, Printers to Her Majesty,
at the Edinburgh University Press.